Global Goals for S[...] Transformation

Volume III: Driving Governance Towards the SDGs

Seema Goyal

walnutpublication.com

INDIA • UK • USA

Paperback ISBN: 979-8-89171-216-4
eBook ISBN: 979-8-89171-217-1

First Published in May, 2025

Published by Walnut Publication

(an imprint of Vyusta Platforms Private Limited)

www.walnutpublication.com

India

Unit# 909, 9th Floor, Wave Silver Tower, Sector-18, Noida - 201301

UK

71-75 Shelton Street, Covent Garden, London, WC2H 9JQ, UK

Distributed by

ZopioTail

This Book is Dedicated to All of You

Acknowledgment

This book is the product of countless conversations, collaborations, and collective insights — and it would not have been possible without the support of many individuals and institutions.

First and foremost, I express my deepest gratitude to all the educators, researchers, and policy leaders whose dedication to sustainable development and social equity continues to inspire this work. Your vision, scholarship, and perseverance laid the foundation for this inquiry.

Thank you for your guidance, your patience, and your unwavering belief in this project. Your insights challenged me to think more deeply and write more clearly.

To the communities, organizations, and field practitioners who generously shared their experiences and time — your stories gave this book its purpose and direction.

To my family and friends, thank you for your encouragement, emotional strength, and the many quiet sacrifices that allowed this work to take shape.

Our many thanks to every reader and changemaker committed to turning Global goals into local action. It is our hope that this work serves not just as a reference, but as a catalyst for continued dialogue, innovation, and transformation.

Finally, I acknowledge the many unsung contributors across sectors — educators in classrooms, students in discussion, policy advocates in negotiation rooms — who work daily to bring the Sustainable Development Goals from vision to reality.

About the Author

Seema Goyal

Educationist | SDG Advocate | Interdisciplinary Researcher | Sustainability Consultant | Founder of SDG Readiness Platform.

Seema Goyal, an Interdisciplinary researcher on SDGs in terms of Education, business and policy making, eager to reimagine the future as a more socially and environmentally just world, committed towards achieving the SDGs. With 20+ years-experience in curriculum design and assess Education sector policies, strategies and programs with a view of ensuring comparability to International best practices, smart solutions and technological advances, and responsiveness to development needs of the country.

We see the purpose of SDG Readiness Platform, as being a catalyst for change that will have an impact. It is a Platform working on SDG's and Climate crisis and aims to leave behind a legacy to inspire people and various stakeholders in this arena about solutions.

Our mission is to get the leaders to meet and learn from each other and be inspired by each other. We want to get this awareness out to millions. This is more than a book, a series of pro-planet book written for everyone –wherever you might be in the world. It is for those who want to easily understand how Climate Change is affecting the planet and who want to make small, simple changes in their everyday lives to become climate aware.

By sharing knowledge, leading by example, and creating spaces for conversation, I've found that I can engage others in meaningful discussions about sustainability. It's a journey that doesn't just involve personal commitment but also empowering others to understand how their actions, whether big or small, can contribute to a more sustainable world.

Gandhi told us to 'be the change we want to see in the world.' This book captures that spirit, reminding us that everyone can do something to help the planet."

Preface

The Missing Link: Exploring the Potential of National Climate Institutions

While much thinking has gone into mechanisms for Global collaboration on Climate Change, National governance is under-studied. Could it be the missing link in accelerating transitions to low-carbon, climate resilient futures?

Why National institutions could be key to spurring climate action

'The Missing Link in Spurring Climate Action?

A spotlight on National climate institutions', solving 'collective action problems' – in this case Climate Change – may not lie in Global negotiations and processes, but in the establishment of specialist domestic institutions that can drive lasting change, even if they are power and resource 'weak'.

The 'top down' approach to tackling Climate Change, revolves around the Conference of Parties (COP) where government representatives and other stakeholders gather to negotiate and agree on an objective – such as the Paris Agreement to limit Global warming to well below 2°C above pre-industrial levels.

Such objectives become the benchmark for collective progress. Capacity and funding support mechanisms are put in place, countries set National goals and actions (their 'Nationally-determined contributions' under the Paris Agreement), and baked in reporting and transparency processes highlight the emissions gaps between what countries have promised and what science says is required to meet the targets.

Conversely, the 'bottom up' approach is can be developed based around things that matter to people and therefore drive the political conversation and political ambition in respective countries.

What's important, is using the domestic context – "these kinds of narratives around daily realities" – to drive policy frameworks and National plans and pathways. And, crucially, National climate institutions can help to bridge these two areas.

"The Global remains important because of collective action, But we can't [tackle Climate Change] because of Global pressures alone.

Countries will ramp it up mostly by the bottom-up approach connecting domestic narratives, political mobilisation, policy frameworks, and institutions, law and regulation.

"We must join together to bring forth a sustainable Global society founded on respect for nature, universal human rights, economic justice, and a culture of peace. Towards this end, it is imperative that we, the peoples of Earth, declare our responsibility to one another, to the greater community of life, and to future generations."

The world is desperately seeking change. People sense that important social, economic and environmental shifts are afoot. There are now over seven billion people on the planet. Technology is helping us to communicate, organise and learn on a Global scale. Emerging economies are rising in all continents and the Global middle class is larger than ever before. Yet inequality between the worlds rich and poor continues to grow, both between and within countries. Extreme weather events are more frequent and severe, and adapting to changes in climate is now a reality. Demand for natural resources is increasing and contributing to the degradation of the environment. food and oil prices set new records and acute debt crises cascade through the Global economy.

"Recognising the Global climate crisis and the need for leaders worldwide to take immediate decisive action to reduce the causes of Climate Change", Governments across the world has to make its mission to provide science-based recommendations for combating the climate crisis and preventing further deterioration. It has to use extensive data, knowledge, and technologies provided by experts in various fields to implement country-specific action plans to be adopted and reinforced by society. Solution pathways in the plan should include elements such as: (1) Existing technologies, (2) Circular economy, (3) Nature-based solutions, (4) Digitalization, (5) Innovation commercialization, (6) Sustainable finance and adaptation investment schemes, and (7) Policy reforms."

- How do we know Climate Change is really happening?

- How much agreement is there among scientists about Climate Change?

- Do we really only have 150 years of climate data?

- How is that enough to tell us about centuries of change?

- How do we know Climate Change is caused by humans?

- Since greenhouse gases occur naturally, how do we know they're causing Earth's temperature to rise?

- Why should we be worried that the planet has warmed 2°F since the 1800s?

- Is Climate Change a part of the planet's natural warming and cooling cycles?

- How do we know Global warming is not because of the sun or volcanoes?

- How can winters and certain places be getting colder if the planet is warming?

- Wildfires and bad weather have always happened. How do we know there's a connection to Climate Change

- How bad are the effects of Climate Change going to be?

- What will it cost to do something about Climate Change, versus doing nothing?

Contents

Chapter 1 – The Domestic Context

Every aspect of government efforts to address Climate Change must be grounded on scientific data. On scientific knowledge and analysis. This is a prerequisite for an effective response to the Climate Change challenges. It is a prerequisite to better understand climate crisis. To better implement policies regarding biodiversity or civil protection. After all, the climate crisis and natural disasters are interrelated. And this is something we cannot ignore.

This should be the philosophy, the approach of the National Climate Institutions: Bridging the "traditional", response-focused risk management approach with the three key pillars:

- Prevention

- Preparedness

- Resilience

These pillars at the "heart" of the approach can be guiding all our actions and initiatives. They can be an integral part of an efficient risk management. They are the compass to put into place a more effective civil protection mechanism. A mechanism which will contribute to enhancing our country's resilience and adaptability. At the core of our efforts lies collaboration. Synergies. Because climate crisis is a complex issue that cannot be efficiently addressed by one country or institution alone. Cooperation is needed.

- Cooperation with the scientific community. Because effective policies and action plans can only be based on scientific data and evidence.

- Cooperation with civil society. Because climate crisis concerns all of us. We are all on the same boat. We must join forces.

- Cooperation with other institutions and agencies. Because the exchange of expertise and best practices is key in addressing climate-related challenges.

- Cooperation at National and International levels like United Nations and agencies UNFCC and UNEP.

"Climate Change brings Global impacts that demand Global solutions. But we also know that governments and companies have a big role to play in driving progress, and that the actions and voices of the citizens really matter,"

As implementation issues come to the fore, National institutions have a greater role to play. They are "no silver bullet", but they haven't been suitably explored or recognised as a catalyst for change.

Where National climate institutions do exist, they have tended to come about as a result of a number of pressures and domestic context drivers.

Traditionally, National climate politics have been influenced by International politics, business interests and civil society and social movements, and then refracted through political institutions, interaction with International processes, and bureaucratic patterns and processes.

India's interaction with International processes on Climate Change, for example, has at times been fractious given that its leaders argue it has only recently become a high emitter of greenhouse gases compared to long-developed countries and that Global expectations threaten to hold it back just as it becomes a major world economy. It may therefore decide to take its cues not from the wider International community, but from China, which is in a similar position.

"Limits to Growth at 50: the groundbreaking study that failed to change the world" 50 years on from the publication of The Limits to Growth, why has its influence on policymakers been so limited? And what can post-growthier learn from the movement that has succeeded in reshaping the world since the 1970s — namely, neoliberalism?

When it was published in 1972, The Limits to Growth was both groundbreaking and controversial. It warned that pursuing infinite growth on a finite planet would lead to collapse. Half a century on, this is no longer a controversial conclusion among scientists. But, in the corridors of power, the notion that never-ending growth might not be desirable — or possible — remains a heresy.

Ten thousand years of human history are crashing into the next three decades, and the Gen Z are the people seeing us through to a sustainable future. How? By working in one of the three GPS fields: sustainable business, policy, or Education - reflect three underlying theories of change: changing the game, changing the rules and fundamentally changing the minds.

The overarching challenge we face is meeting the needs of eight, soon to be nine, soon to be ten billion people on this one earth, where half the folks alive are barely getting by on a few dollars a day, and almost everyone wants to consume more. Where we are already fighting over water, oil, topsoil, fish, forests, biodiversity. Where economic systems across the world are rooted in the legacy injustices of genocide, slavery, and colonization. And where it is getting hotter year after year after year.

At the same time, there has never been a more exciting, decisive, more human time to be alive. No generations before us have had the tools, social networks, shared understandings, technologies and business models to stabilize the climate and profoundly change the future. We can clearly see two paths, and the road to a sustainable society and a circular economy remains open, leading the change: rewiring the world with clean energy, redesigning cities across the earth, reimagining the Global food system, reinventing transportation, regenerating prairies, forests and oceans.

The Paris Goal is a Physical limit, not a political choice. Today's action will shape life on Earth for centuries. What we say and do in this moment, how we vote and act, will decide if we have a Livable Planet.

Action on Climate Change will only really be driven at the National level. National political shifts, backed by narratives and institutions, are really the primary driver of change in country after country. Global cooperation is important, but it cannot be the main driver of change. The pushing of either mitigation or embedded narratives is really important. Build climate institutions that match National politics and National context.

All of this points to the importance of states and state capacity, but not necessarily in a crude way where you have to set very big, ambitious targets and big machinery, but nimble, creative and flexible opportunities to accelerate the cycle between politics and institutions is what will drive National action, and ultimately help us address this problem.

Why does this Matter?

- While digital technologies offer large productivity payoffs, they also create new challenges, especially for developing countries still catching up on technological shifts. To benefit from the advantages of digital transformation, economic policy needs to ensure that it does not increase inequality. Left unchecked, industrial concentration and inhibitive market structures dominated by some countries/firms may impede a wider technology adoption to lift aggregate productivity and foster more robust economic growth.

- Apart from leveraging digitalization for effective public governance, governments must keep pace with the ever-evolving technologies and shifting skills demands in labour markets.

Three Pathways to Sustainability

Change Minds through Education. Change the Rules through Policy. And Change the Game through Business. The world needs leaders driving each of these strategies for change.

Theory of Change:

Changing the rules—using policy to attack social and environmental problems—has a well-known justification in economics. Environmental pollution and resource degradation, as well as social exploitation, are considered by economists to be negative externalities—costs that arise in the production of goods and services that are not borne by the consumer or producer.

Because these costs are not embedded in the cost or price of the goods, there is no incentive to reduce them—and so firms over-pollute, and treat workers, suppliers and communities unfairly. Under the traditional thinking it is hard for any individual company to address these problems, as it would raise their costs and put them at a competitive disadvantage.

To increase the overall well-being of society, government needs to step in and level the playing field, requiring all firms for example to reduce pollution, provide transparent product information, or prevent bribery or slave labor in their supply chains. While sustainable business has recently started to shift this paradigm, still, for many environmental and social problems, government action remains critical.

Never waste a crisis as Milton Friedman famously observed:

"Only a crisis — actual or perceived — produces real change. When that crisis occurs, the actions that are taken depend on the ideas that are lying around. That, I believe, is our basic function: to develop alternatives to existing policies, to keep them alive and available until the politically impossible becomes the politically inevitable." –

Defining a New Economic Paradigm on Wellbeing and Happiness

Regenerative journey - Alternative Economics! Maybe you're unsure of how you or your community can make an impact on the economy but understanding that the way we work and spend money, all play a part in creating the economy. We can empower ourselves to seek alternative solutions and change our habits.

- Have you ever thought about how our current Global Economic System just isn't sustainable?

- Have you wondered what alternatives are out there?

- Do you want to learn what the true meaning of wealth and economy are? Or maybe you have your own project and want help creating a business plan?

How we can Re-Design these Economic Systems

Because after all, to do nothing is to accept that the answer to our problems is more economic growth – more production, more consumption, more highways, more buildings, more logging, more fishing, etc. This degenerative cycle of continuous growth is not sustainable. Let's flip the switch and change to a more circular economy, one centred around gift-giving, well-being and equality.

- To assess the impact of the Global economy in your projects

- To find out economic opportunities in your projects and develop them within the model of a social enterprise

- To understand how to create a complementary currency

- To create a business plan for your projects

- To find ethical financial opportunities for your projects

- Explore how Economics is not a science, it is a system designed by humans; therefore, it is open to redesign Why Do We Need New Voices in Public Policy?

- How do policy processes have to change to rebuild trust and enable power sharing at all levels of environmental decision making, implementation and monitoring?

Why Do We Need New Voices in Public Policy?

This is a crucial decade for tackling the nature crisis, and policy ambition, action, and cooperation at Global and National scales critical to success. It is time to support Researchers, scientists, policy-makers to take action for people and planet. Their experience and expertise can support governments in the development and implementation of biodiversity policy, in the context of National, regional, and intergovernmental agreements and processes, to design and use tools, such as biodiversity indicators and National ecosystem assessments, to meet National and Internationally established biodiversity-related goals and targets. The integration of nature through the UN Common Approach to biodiversity, and the delivery of various biodiversity-related multilateral environmental agreements, including the framework on Convention on Biological Diversity.

The profiles, backgrounds, and demographics of Researchers, public policy professionals often fail to reflect the growing pluralism and multiculturalism of our societies. How can the inclusion of diverse voices help to reimagine and redesign the future of public policy in ways that are more equitable, inclusive, and effective?

Achieving meaningful progress on diversity and equity in public policy is one of the most significant Global imperatives of our time, permeating every geography and culture, and every sector and profession.

To build a leadership pipeline and increase diversity in the field, more must be done to ensure public policy is an inclusive and viable career path for minorities, and to create opportunities for emerging and new voices in public policy to practice leadership through their projects, institutions, and communities.

Beyond Changing the Rules

The way through to a sustainable future requires policy change at all levels—local, state, National, UN, corporate, and in non-profit organizations and government agencies. To meet the needs of nine to ten billion people, we also need to change minds through Education and change the game through sustainable business.

The Challenge of Climate Science

To support the transformation in the fields of sustainable development, environmental economics, green finance, corporate social responsibility and transformative policies.

The problem of Climate Change is becoming one of the great historical problems of our era. Climate Change has a Global reach and a pervasive influence on all sectors of our society. The problem of Climate Change is becoming one of the great historical problems of our era.

Climate Change has a Global reach and a pervasive influence on all sectors of our society. It is a threat to economic well-being, to an equilibrated and sustainable path to development for emerging economies and to the equilibrium of the mature economies. The recently acquired capability of mankind to change our environment is posing unprecedented issues for complexity and outreach.

Climate Change is also strongly science-based. The base for this debate is rooted in sophisticated scientific arguments derived by using advanced numerical methods and techniques. This fact poses a special responsibility on the climate scientific community: we have to respond to society demands for information that has to be accurate, honest and timely.

We can easily convince ourselves of the extreme complexity of the climate system, a system that contains unknown or poorly known processes, strong nonlinear interactions that enhance sensitivity to small perturbation. How is it possible a quantitative scientific consideration of such a system? This is the great challenge that climate science is facing today, to obtain a scientific method that will produce assessments that will be reliable, consistent and quantitative. The main tool to respond to this challenge is the numerical circulation models of climate. The numerical approach to climate will be presented with a review of recent results and a critical assessment of its potential and limitations.

Biodiversity is facing unprecedented threats. Yet, the financial sector is only just beginning to step up, with biodiversity funds and initiatives gaining traction to protect nature while driving innovation and opportunity.

Key insights:

- Over 50% of Global GDP relies on nature, but current investments in biodiversity fall massively short of what's needed to reverse the decline by 2030.

- Solutions are emerging, from regenerative agriculture to habitat banks, and new funding models that aim to address biodiversity loss AND create opportunities for investors.

- Clear regulatory frameworks are needed for scaling up efforts and turn intention into impactful action.

As Sir David Attenborough said, "Bringing economics and ecology together, we can help save the natural world at what may be the last minute."

- To achieve the Sustainable Development Agenda, our economies must urgently transform to respond to existing and emerging challenges, away from the conventional understanding of simply driving GDP growth.

- We need to reconsider how we valorize economic well-being. Well-being and progress need to be measured not just in economic terms alone but also in terms of the true cost incurred by nature and society.

- The transformation required to achieve the Sustainable Development Goals is a multi-dimensional process in which growth or progress balances the three dimensions of sustainable development — social, environmental and economic.

- We speak a lot about Climate Change, but also about biodiversity, about toxic substances or about water. And we really need to act. And what drove this crossing of the planetary boundaries?

- Well, it's the race for profits, this dogma of growth that is supposed to bring all the happiness in the world. What we've been told for ages is it's supposed to bring us a redistribution of wealth. So, social equality. It's also supposed to bring us to technologies that would save the environment that we are destroying. And it's supposed to solve all our problems.

- So, everyone is just running after growth. Whether it be private companies wanting to chase profits they need as growth, and political leaders that also pretend that chasing this growth is going to solve all the issues that we have. And we can definitely see that this is not working, that we are crossing these planetary boundaries, putting at risk the survival of humanity and of many other species and not solving the issue of social inequality.

- Well, for a few decades, we have believed that somehow, we could keep growing and polluting less at the same time, we call it 'green growth'. We talked of decoupling the two, but now, science has shown us with hundreds of studies that actually decoupling is not happening.

So right now, we have this obsession with GDP, which is a 100-year-old indicator, which is a bit strange because it's completely decorrelated to well-being in high-income countries, but we're also facing the unsustainability of the pursuit of growth.

So degrowth basically is a plan B. We've tried green growth. That's not going to work now. I think that should be acknowledged as a fact as a result of the latest IPCC report. And so, we do need to organise a democratically planned downscaling of production and consumption in high-income countries and organise it so that it can be done in a way that is both equitable and convivial.

Chapter 2 - Disruptive Megatrends and Economic Challenges

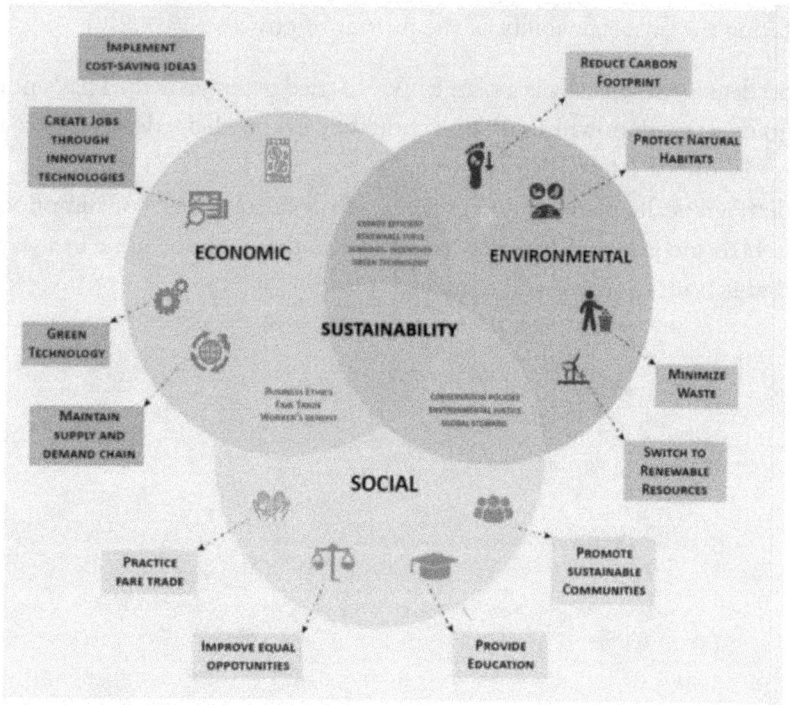

We live in times of extreme change – and the changes occur across multiple domains, each having profound implications for the systems we have created for society, the environment, and economies.

Let's look at megatrends that need us to rethink how we approach economic development and collective welfare.

1. Living in a progressively warming planet - increase in Global temperature is the most pressing policy issue today and has been for the last decade. Today, the effects of Global warming can already be seen in the shape of droughts, floods, and erratic

weather patterns. Their impacts on human lives and livelihoods and the increasing socio-economic costs they inflict on National economies are forcing governments, the private sector, and citizens to pay more attention to the threat of Climate Change. Failure to take immediate action will lead us to a tipping point where changes to the climate become irreversible.

2. The 2007 report of the IPCC highlighted the need to restrict Global warming to 1.5 degrees. Crossing this threshold will lead to progressive losses of life and well-being of millions of people in the decades ahead. Even if all emissions from human activities cease today, carbon dioxide already in the atmosphere will remain there for about 40 years. Irrespective of our future emissions, we will face the economic, human and environmental costs of past inaction. While we may not entirely escape the costs of earlier inaction, mitigating Climate Change presents unprecedented opportunities for the Global economy and societies if we act decisively now.

3. Increasing population, varying composition - As countries see an increase in their fertility rates, they will also see an increase in the share of the working-age population in the future. This is called the 'demographic dividend'. As overall dependency ratios fall, more resources become available to increase investments in Education, health, employment, social protection, pension schemes, etc., fostering short and medium-term economic growth and well-being. Countries at an early stage of the demographic transition can maximize the benefits of the dividend by investing in human capital formation through investments in Education and health, progress toward gender equality, and job creation.

4. Gearing up for Rapid Urbanisation- Given its breadth and scope, urbanization is arguably the most complex megatrend. It spans issues of structural transformation of economies,

environmental sustainability, inclusion and poverty eradication. The process by which a country shifts from primarily rural to mainly urban has implications for agriculture, industry and services and how these can be combined to transform the economy. When capital, labour, technology and talent agglomerate in urban areas, countries can kickstart innovation, boost productivity and use resources sustainably while creating markets for fresh and locally processed foods that stimulate agriculture crucial to rural livelihoods. But if not done well, urbanization results in urban sprawls, stress on urban ecosystems and infrastructure, crowding out of human capital and enterprise from rural economies, unemployment and environmental distress.

5. Keeping pace with the technological shifts - The combination of digitalization with transformative technological breakthroughs is unleashing social and economic structural shifts that are long-term and irreversible, with far-reaching consequences – both positive and negative – for humanity. The ongoing wave of technological change is transforming labour markets on multiple fronts. Technological progress has caused job losses over the past two centuries. Still, it has also helped create jobs, many in new sectors and industries that considerably impact the size and shape of an economy.

6. As technology adoption costs fall and the demand for skills and jobs changes in response, countries need to find new growth opportunities. These shifts are also enabling Global connectivity like never before. However, digital transformation could also exacerbate inequality. Concerted action at Global and local levels to bridge the digital divide will create avenues for new participants in economic value chains, entrepreneurship and inclusion.

Interdisciplinary Approaches to Improve Decision-Making

Reimagining Educational Multilateralism - with a multistakeholder, interdisciplinary insight network designed to address critical Global challenges through transformative ideas. It can consist of 30 councils made up of experts across business, government, academia and civil society, from UN member countries, who can be nominated for two-year terms.

Mission

The Network can help to identify and disseminate transformative ideas with the potential for Global impact. The Global Future Council members can provide strategic insights, scientific evidence, forward guidance, and multidisciplinary understanding of major issues through:

- Fresh ideas and innovative thinking: Nurturing cutting-edge and disruptive ideas and developing the foresight to identify and shape key areas

- Grounding in expertise and evidence: Providing a foundation for data-, evidence-, fact- and research-based public-private cooperation

- Interdisciplinary and systems approach: Connecting the dots between established and frontier issues and integrating thought leaders from business, academia, civil society, government and International organizations

Councils play two types of roles – Frontier exploration to address cutting-edge themes that have transformative potential, infuse new ideas, connect frontier thinkers and serve as test beds for future workstreams; and, systems thinking to contribute in a meaningful way to complex Global discussions and issues where a multistakeholder group of constituents can drive positive systemic change.

As Global environmental challenges accumulate, the necessity for cooperation and effective multilateral institutions becomes increasingly evident. Despite the inception of the contemporary environmental governance system five decades ago, and the subsequent growth of involved institutions and commitments, environmental challenges persist and escalate. The 2022 UN report titled "A Breakthrough for People and Planet" underscores the imperative of revitalizing faith in multilateralism and highlighting the environment within this framework.

- The value of interdisciplinary and multistakeholder solutions to economic, technological, societal and environmental challenges in the face of geopolitical and economic uncertainty.

- The cross-cutting program addressed harnessing artificial intelligence, accelerating the green transition, reviving productivity, addressing antimicrobial resistance and stabilizing trade.

- 30 councils to develop proposals for collaboration that can create transformative change in the next three years in each of their topic areas.

- In a world marked by division, bringing people together from different disciplines, sectors and geographies to consider new and different views and find pathways for agreement has never been more essential to exchange insights and advance solutions to interconnected challenges facing the world.

On Building Trust for Global Collaboration

- From debating models of economic growth to examining the increasing effects of advancing artificial intelligence (AI) to outlining sustainable approaches to climate action and nature protection, the experts from business, government, academia and civil society aligned on shared risks, highlighted new opportunities and committed to continuing constructive, inclusive dialogue and designing proposals for collaboration.

- It's important to answer new questions in areas such as digital transformation, geopolitical and Climate Changes, economic and social transformations, space, and advanced science and technology - more "difficult conversations" about how to tackle challenging

- Trade-offs, such as between decarbonization and sustainable development, increased productivity and job disruption, and competition and collaboration.

- Investment in sustainability is not a trade-off for business, but is actually a trade-on. It's about having a green mindset and shifting your perspective."

- The ideas, insights and approaches to problem-solving and cross-cutting sessions are key to creating and advancing the public-private collaboration that is necessary to address the deeply interconnected issues of today.

- Testing ideas, challenging each other and fostering collective creativity will lay the foundations for new innovations and multistakeholder partnerships to meet the demands of the future."

- With recent geopolitical shocks, economic uncertainty, technological and societal shifts, and increased fragmentation, we have arguably entered "a new era,".

Climate Litigation is on the rise- No Place to Hide

Achieving the SDGs is not up to countries alone. It will require deep transformations at the local level—transformations in transportation, energy, urban planning, and access to public services such as health and Education. SDSN estimates that about two-thirds (65%) of the

169 targets underlying the 17 SDGs can only be reached with the proper engagement of, and coordination with, local and regional governments. Cities, in particular, have a crucial role to play in achieving the SDGs, as UN-Habitat estimates that around one third of all SDG indicators have a local or urban component, and the UN estimates that nearly 5 billion people will live in towns or cities by 2030.

Regional cooperation is also essential, as countries who share borders, cultures, economies, and natural features such as transboundary waterways, must collaborate to enact positive transformations that will affect them all.

I don't think enough people understand that it is not just roads, bridges, Buildings, Housing systems and water systems that aren't designed to present climate conditions.

But it is also mental health systems, insurance systems, agricultural systems, Emergency relief preparedness and medical Education systems.

More than 50% of climate cases have direct judicial outcomes that can be understood as favorable to climate action. Climate cases continue to have significant indirect impacts on Climate Change decision-making beyond the courtroom, too. In addition, there has been growth in climate-washing cases challenging the accuracy of green claims and commitments. Litigation concerning investment decisions is also increasing and can help clarify the parameters within which decisions should be made in the context of Climate Change.

As reiterated, climate litigation is commonly associated with pro-regulatory (climate-aligned) cases aimed at advancing climate action and anti-regulatory (non-climate-aligned) cases seeking to delay or obstruct climate action. However, the just-transition litigation: cases that aim to strike a balance between advancing the transition to a low-carbon economy with protecting the rights of affected communities, highlighting the complex interests and needs involved in the transition process.

In sum, numerous new developments suggest that climate litigation is having an impact both within and beyond the courtroom. The overall body of direct outcomes in Global climate cases tilted in favor of climate action, and also new stakeholders engaging with the phenomenon of litigation.

The future trends, predicting increasing litigation focuses on the following issues:

- Litigation focused on the biodiversity, climate nexus particularly arguing that more ambitious measures are needed to restore forests and enhance their carbon absorption capacities;

- Future cases addressing the duties of governments and corporations to protect the ocean from further climate impacts and to explore ocean acidification and ocean-based carbon dioxide removal techniques

- Litigation arising from extreme weather events where Climate Change may not be the central focus, but where cases can still have significant implications for climate action

- Cases concerning short-lived climate pollutants, such as methane and black carbon soot, which are identified by scientists as crucial targets for mitigation

- International litigation between states, particularly regarding disputes over fossil fuel production and use.

Let us all celebrate what is right in order to find the energy to fix what is wrong. Act Now is the United Nations campaign to inspire people to act for the Sustainable Development Goals.

The Goals can improve life for all of us. Cleaner air. Safer cities. Equality. Better jobs. These issues matter to everyone. But progress is too slow. We have to act, urgently, to accelerate changes that add up to better lives on a healthier planet."

What tools and services support effective implementation, monitoring and enforcement at the country level?

How are public-private partnerships, leadership coalitions, and civil society innovations changing the policy, finance, and business landscape, and transforming production and consumption worldwide?

Mainstreaming Climate Change and disaster risk reduction in urban and rural planning to achieve the SDGs

Climate Change and escalating disaster risks necessitate the integration of these factors into planning frameworks to cultivate resilient communities and attain the SDGs. Research into the fundamental interconnections among Climate Change adaptation, disaster risk reduction, and sustainable development, emphasizing the incorporation of Climate Change and disaster risk reduction considerations into planning processes.

Examine exemplary practices, innovative strategies, and case studies across diverse geographic contexts, elucidating effective methods for integrating Climate Change and disaster risk considerations into both urban and rural planning. Additionally, research on topics such as enhancing infrastructure resilience, promoting ecosystem-based adaptation, fostering community engagement, and utilizing technology and data-driven approaches for informed decision-making is required at all governance levels - Local, Regional and National.

Chapter 3 - Future of Work and Jobs for Green Economy

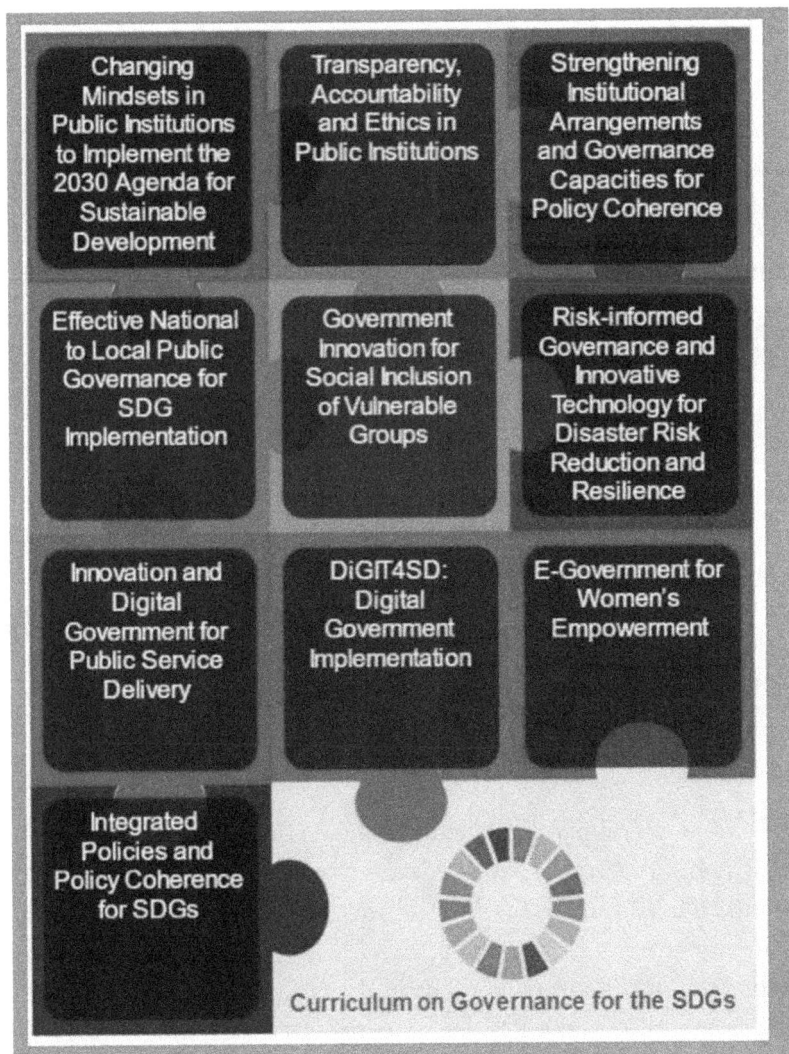

Changing Mindsets in Public Institutions to Implement the 2030 Agenda for Sustainable Development	Transparency, Accountability and Ethics in Public Institutions	Strengthening Institutional Arrangements and Governance Capacities for Policy Coherence
Effective National to Local Public Governance for SDG Implementation	Government Innovation for Social Inclusion of Vulnerable Groups	Risk-informed Governance and Innovative Technology for Disaster Risk Reduction and Resilience
Innovation and Digital Government for Public Service Delivery	DiGIT4SD: Digital Government Implementation	E-Government for Women's Empowerment
Integrated Policies and Policy Coherence for SDGs		

Curriculum on Governance for the SDGs

There is a massive shift underway in the Global economy. There is a massive shift underway in the Global economy. In the wake of the pandemic, the world is witnessing a historic transformation in how people work, why they work and where they work. It is called the Great Reshuffle, an unprecedented moment in history where we are reimagining the future of work. People are actively acquiring new skills and pursuing new ventures. Employers are reinventing business models and creating new markets. And all of this economic upheaval, which would normally play out over the course of decades, is being compressed into a couple of years.

Amid this Great Reshuffle, we're faced with an urgent need to transition our society to a green economy to address the threat of Climate Change. How do we apply what we've learned from this unprecedented moment to power the enormous transition that needs to happen to meet the climate crisis?

Achieving our collective Global climate targets is a monumental task and it is going to take a whole- of-economy effort to make it happen. That means we need a transformation in the skills and jobs people have if we're going to get there. The good news is that we are already seeing a shift to green skills and jobs underway on various Online platform and higher Education institutions. Green talent in the workforce worldwide is rising. The share of green talent increased from 9.6% in 2015, to 13.3% so far in 2021 (a growth rate of 38.5%).

Jobs are a critical part of the conversation about achieving this green transition. And rightly so. We expect to see millions of new jobs created Globally in the next decade driven by new climate policies and commitments. For example, in the last five years, the number of Renewables & Environment jobs in the U.S. has increased by 237%, in stark contrast to the 19% increase for Oil & Gas jobs.

At this pace, the Renewables & Environment sector will outnumber Oil & Gas in total jobs on our platform by 2030.

It's more than jobs — we need to zoom in on the skills that power these jobs. Green skills. We believe real change will come through skills- based approach to opportunity. We have seen double-digit growth across dozens of green skills over the last five years. The fastest-growing green skills are in Ecosystem Management, Environmental Policy and Pollution Prevention. But the vast majority of green skills are being used in jobs that aren't traditionally thought of as green — such as fleet managers, data scientists or health workers.

Governments, companies, and individuals all need to come together to help transition the hiring market from focusing solely on titles and companies, degrees and schools, to also focusing on skills and abilities. Government and businesses should become a catalyst for job and skill transformations, and provide the tools to help.

Policymakers Action Plan: Champion green skills and prepare the workforce for the green transition

- Take a skills-based approach to opportunity to pave the way for real change. Connect green skills, jobs and broader green economy policies, ensuring development is balanced with demand and the pace of transformation in the marketplace. Provide clarity and direction on which skills need to be developed and the types of training that will be available to prepare for the future.

- Adopt a targeted approach to progressively focus green upskilling and reskilling efforts in a given location. Integration of these insights into awareness-raising and Education settings should be made a priority. Partner with experts to build training materials and promote online learning resources to equip not only entrepreneurs but also the wider community with the necessary green skills to boost employability throughout the green transition. Provide investment into training, including empowering and fostering entrepreneurship. Channel efforts into growing these bridging skillsets to accelerate the transition.

- Ensure new policies create opportunities for the equal development of green skills across all groups, supported by significant investment to ensure green- skilling opportunities are accessible to diverse groups. Consider the influence of external factors in creating potential skill discrepancies to protect vulnerable groups, then remove potential barriers, convene discussion, enable knowledge sharing and pool resources.

Business leaders and Governments together must Invest in upskilling current and future green talent

- Support green upskilling and reskilling efforts through targeted investment into workforce training, through learning courses and local programs.

- Hire diverse talent with green skills.

- Recognize the importance of green hiring and upskilling on your talent brand — current employees and prospective candidates expect their employers to take action on Climate Change.

- Reimagine some open and future roles — the vast majority of green skills are being used in jobs that aren't traditionally thought of as green.

- Find or fund entrepreneurial opportunities that will help individuals identify green business opportunities, expand economies and increase green skills intensity in your sector or others.

To complement government efforts, systemic corporate investments in skilling could play a decisive role in attracting larger investments at the National level. Corporations could consider industry level collaborations to provide industry specific skills. This would be a CSR investment with a substantial social return, while adding to the availability of quality manpower for their respective sectors. During this decade, India Inc. can play a catalytic role in increasing the availability of skilled manpower in the country.

VET and the Green Transition: What are the skills and Education needed for finance professionals to play their part?

Managing the impact of people on the planet we call home, has become the rallying call of our times. As governments around the world are seeking to define a vision for decarbonizing their economies and achieving net zero emissions, there is an urgent need for all stakeholders to grasp the scale of this challenge and to respond to it.

In too many organizations however, expertise in climate risk and ESG still resides in a small group of sustainability experts; this must change rapidly and become embedded in organizations' culture. There is a pressing need to raise the level of knowledge and understanding, both to recognize Climate Change as an urgent 'burning platform' – and to respond accordingly.

Finance professionals and professional accountants have a critical role in putting sustainability at the heart of decision-making, and in championing responsible practices that will drive the critical changes the planet needs, both to lead long-term value creation within sustainable economies, and to champion responsible practices in the public interest.

And to make sure they have proper tools at their disposal to do so, they must be equipped with the right Education and skills.

The time for action is now. Governments, companies and individuals have to come together to address the urgent climate crisis. Policymakers, business leaders and the Global workforce have a shared opportunity and responsibility.

Achieving our climate targets is a monumental task and it is going to take a whole-of-economy effort to make it happen. That means we need a transformation in the skills and jobs people have if we're going to get there.

Green skills are the core of the green transition and harnessing the shift of talent. Through a targeted approach, we can progressively shift towards these greener jobs, using skills to identify jobs with the highest ability to turn sectors and countries green. We need more opportunities for those with green skills, we have to upskill workers who currently lack those skills, and we need to ensure green skills are hardwired into the skillset of future generations.

Potential Policy Response

FIGURE 1.1.

Five-module foresight process to stress-test public policy

EXPLORE DISRUPTIONS
Examine key assumptions and identify possible disruptions in the global, regional and national context

IMAGINE INTERACTIONS
Explore possible implications that would occur if two or more disruptions occur simultaneously

CREATE SCENARIOS
Develop alternative future scenarios based on selected disruptions from the workshops

ENVISION AND STRATEGISE
Develop strategies for successful public policy under each alternative scenario

RECOMMEND POLICIES
Identify cross-cutting implications and develop scenario-agnostic actions to strengthen current policies

Given the possibility that information campaigns could target climate strategies, governments should integrate misinformation and disinformation risk assessments into all major climate initiatives and implementation plans. To mitigate the risks, governments should invest proactively in communications plans for climate initiatives to push the widespread adoption of sustainable products and behavioral changes.

Governments must be prepared to take rapid large-scale action to meet climate targets or respond to catastrophic weather events, exploring ways to grow their legitimacy to act in case large-scale behavioral change policies are needed.

Buy-in and understanding could be built through tools such as citizens' assemblies and supported through a public narrative focusing on green jobs and the wartime-like mobilization necessary to address the climate emergency.

How governments can use SDG financing strategies to strengthen linkages between different approaches to SDG budgeting, medium-term revenue strategies and private investment for sustainable development. Aim to bring together insights and lessons from countries where the INFF approach has been adopted, and to shed light on innovations that governments can pursue to strengthen their national financing architectures in service of inclusive cities and sustainable development.

Government officials can work in relation to:

- The value added and practicalities of implementing integrated approach for financing the SDGs

- Key innovation and policy solution being pursued in the context of integrated approaches to financing Domestic Revenue Mobilisation for the SDGs

- Budgeting for Social Sectors

- Climate Change and Green Dimensions of Budgeting for the SDGs

- Budgeting for Gender Equality and Inclusion

- Integrated National Financing Frameworks and Financing the SDGs

- Budget Transparency and Accountability for Sustainable Development

- Technical Assistance and capacity building

Climate Change and Sustainable Development Department (CCSD) can lead the development of policy, strategy, operational plans, guidelines and knowledge products. The Department can become responsible for thematic areas like: (i) Climate Change and resilience, covering Climate Change, disaster risk management, and environmental sustainability; (ii) gender; (iii) transition states and engagement; (iv) digital technology for development (v) regional cooperation integration (RCI) and trade.

Chapter 4 – What is a Skills Friendly City?

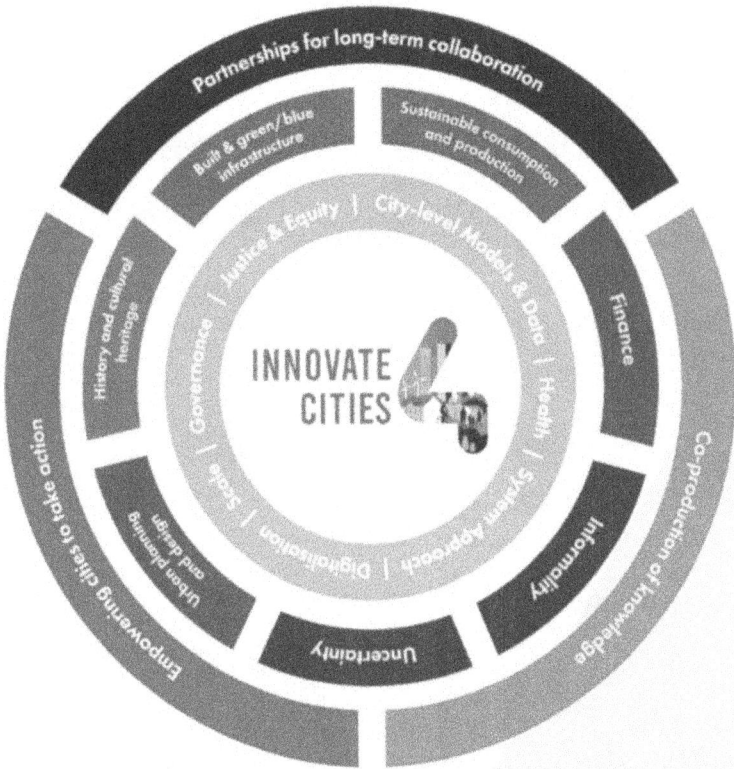

The Skills Friendly City initiative outlines ten standards needed to create a "skills friendly" city, including critical activities and indicators of success that lead to a better-prepared generation of youth ready to enter the workforce.

Skills Friendly Cities are working to build more equitable and effective skills enabling environments for young people, at the local level, alongside the business community, Education institutions and youth. They strive for conditions and collaboration among actors to positively impact a young person's ability to acquire relevant skills or a quality job. A skills friendly city fully cultivates a collaborative ecosystem for young people ages 15-25 encompassing (1) Education and training; (2) public policies and public sector efforts; (3) employers; (4) connections and matchmaking between jobseekers and employers; (5) funding and investment from public, private and other actors.

Cities to develop bold, innovative ideas that equip young people with skills to participate in the workforce and address the standards (see below) for a Skills Friendly City.

Historical insights to shape livable cities -

- Blending modernity with cultural and natural heritage in urban spaces.

- The power of storytelling to make dense information and research accessible.

- The importance of community bonds and leadership in fostering environmental stewardship.

Inclusive Cities for All

- How cities can be impacted by Climate Change and contribute to it through human activities and infrastructure.

- Express the multitude of scalable, impactful mitigation and adaptation solutions that can be deployed in cities and towns across the world to ensure a climate-ready future.

- Deepen one's understanding of the people and institutions instrumental to the development of urban climate strategies, policies, and financing.

- Expand one's professional network and skills to apply urban climate mitigation and adaptation solutions.

- How do cities of the past guide us toward a better urban future?

- What can citizens do to build accountable and responsive city leadership?

- How does the rise in urbanization impact sustainable development? How does it impact specific areas of sustainable development such as land-use change, Global emissions, social equity and more?

- How does Globalization and the increasing interconnection of societies and trade across the world affect the growth of mega-cities?

- Think about your city. What energy system does your city currently run on, and what would it take to convert your city's infrastructure to clean, green electricity?

- Think about your home or work environment. Imagine a system governed by the Internet of Things. How could you make the appliances and features of that living space work together to create a smarter, greener system?

- What can be done to make cities more healthful spaces? Could more parks and plants help to decrease carbon in the atmosphere to make the air more breathable? Can mass public transport and travel by bicycle be encouraged to increase physical activity and decrease pollution?

- How can coastal cities prepare for environmental changes such as sea-level rise and increased extreme weather?

- How can cities work together to create clean energy systems and lower greenhouse gas emissions?

- In addition to lowering greenhouse gas emissions, how can mass public transport and the share-economy contribute to economic and social inclusion?

- How can cities, as mixed-use environments, continue to foster the growth of universities and similar centers of learning and innovation? Why are these knowledge centers found most often in urban settings? What does this mean for the development of sustainable cities?

- How can the internet and the network of e-Everything connect these centers of innovation to create more sustainable solutions across larger physical and social distances? How can this collaboration help to achieve the goals of social inclusion, economic prosperity, and environmental sustainability?

- Explain how can we get to a zero-carbon energy system.

Environmental

Three different discussion topics: (1) how we move and get around (sustainable mobility); (2) how we make energy green and fair (sustainable energy); (3) and how we eat and consume (sustainable food and consumption). For each thematic module, focus on two key questions.

Figure 14: Derivation of the ESG categories

Category	Commonly defined criteria	ESG categories used in the mapping exercise
Environmental	• climate mitigation • climate adaptation • pollution prevention • biodiversity • water • circular economy	• E - climate mitigation • E - climate adaptation • E - pollution prevention • E - biodiversity • E - water • E - circular economy
Social	• decent work • adequate living standards • wellbeing for end-use • inclusive and sustainable communities and societies	• S - health and safety • S - employees • S - community impact
Governance	• strategy • governance • compliance • risk management system	• G - strategy • G - governance • G - compliance • G - risk management • G - economic information

How are organizations using energy and managing their environmental impacts as stewards of the planet? Examples: carbon emissions, Climate Change effects, pollution, waste disposal, renewable energy, resource depletion.

Social

How are organizations fostering people and culture, and what kind of impact does that have on the community? Examples: supply chain, discrimination, political contributions, diversity, human rights, community relations

Governance

How are organizations directed and controlled, and how are leaders held accountable? Examples: executive compensation, shareholders' rights, takeover defense, staggered boards, independent directors, board elections

- How well do you understand, measure and report the true environmental and social impacts of your organization?

- How rigorously do you champion a diverse, equitable and inclusive workplace?

- In what ways do you embrace and promote a culture of transparency?

- How do you involve stakeholders in strategic planning, dialogue and decision-making processes?

- How boldly do you collaborate beyond your organization? Beyond business?

With all the above factors in mind, why are SDGs so important for local and regional governments?

1. The SDGs provide a shared narrative of sustainable development and help guide the public's understanding of

complex challenges.

2. The SDGs provide an integral framework for sustainable development at the local level.

3. Be involved in the Global community.

4. The commitment of LRGs to the Global agenda promotes their recognition and legitimation as key actors of the Global sustainable development system.

5. The recognition of LRGs as key actors for sustainable development enables them to claim for better political and economic frameworks at National level.

6. The 2030 Agenda recognizes LRG leadership at territorial level and their capacity to articulate territorial stakeholders for sustainable development.

7. Mobilize domestic and International financial resources for sustainable local development.

8. Look for capacity building initiatives focusing on the reinforcement of LRGs' operative and institutional capacities.

9. The SDGs reinforce statistical institutions specialized in collecting data at local and regional level.

10. The SDGs serve as a roadmap for decentralized cooperation between the LRGs.

Why are Local and Regional Governments (LRGs) Important for the SDGs?

City and county governments have long been at the forefront of climate action, advancing bold policies and engaging communities despite inconsistent federal leadership. Yet, climate communication has not always been a priority for local staff stretched thin by tight budgets. That is starting to change. Increasingly, local government leaders recognize that climate communication is a vital climate strategy. How do they listen to their communities? How do they frame climate action to resonate across diverse communities? How can behavior change campaigns scale the impact? What strategies help them turn constituent feedback into tangible progress?

From the initiation stages of the SDGs, it is clear that localizing the SDGs is important to take into account subnational and local contexts in the achievement of the SDGs, from the setting of goals and targets, to determining the means of implementation and using indicators to measure and monitor progress.

Localizing SDGs also means putting local areas and peoples' priorities, needs and resources at the center of sustainable development. Discussions pointed to a need for sustained exchanges between the Global, National and local levels to achieve the SDGs.

The achievement of all SDGs requires local action –

All the SDGs have a local dimension that is essential to their achievement. Local political leaders, with a direct mandate from citizens, have a responsibility to contribute to the achievement of all of the SDGs. Acknowledging the vital role of local and regional governments in the achievement of the agenda will enable us to mobilize local stakeholders and to create new partnerships, based on a common understanding of our shared humanity. Local governments and their associations need to be strengthened to engage in the implementation process, both in the definition and implementation. All local governments need to have the means and the capacity to improve administration, anticipate demands, plan and implement solutions. Peer-to-peer review among local governments has proven to be a very effective way of achieving strengthened local governments.

LRGs play a key role in developing integrated urban and territorial plans to localize all the SDGs –

LRGs build their capacities and engaging in a long-term vision to integrate the SDGs into their strategic local frameworks (e.g. local plans for the 2030 Agenda) as well as their daily activities.

LRGs can be proactive in sharing, learning and developing more holistic and comprehensive participatory plans at the urban and territorial level (e.g. 'strategic planning', city development strategies, etc.). These use cross-cutting policies to respond simultaneously to all the SDGs. Integrated urban and territorial plans promote place-based approaches to development, and they foster multilevel and multi-Sectoral systems of governance, while at the same time promoting alignment with the SDGs.

- LRGs lead innovative actions to achieve Goals and Targets that are instrumental to the 'transformation towards sustainable and resilient societies

- LRGs with an enabling institutional framework play a key role in integrating social housing and neighborhood improvement at the heart of local policies.

- Local governments are policy makers and catalysts of change at the local level and are best placed to link the Global goals with local communities

- As the level of government, the closest of the citizens, cities and regions are where transformations towards more effective, accountable and transparent institutions must begin.

- Localizing SDGs is then a process to empower all local stakeholders, aimed at making sustainable development more responsive, and therefore, relevant to local needs and aspirations. SDGs can be achieved only if local actors fully participate, not only in the implementation, but also in the agenda-setting and monitoring.

- LRGs operate at the level of government which is closest to citizens and, as such, have direct responsibilities in the achievement of the different dimensions of SDG 16, which is an enormous task.

- LRGs play an important role in the delivery of public services The provision of vital infrastructure, and establishing an administrative context and conditions that are conducive to business and/ or providing a socio-economic environment that favours growth and productivity (SDG 8.2).

- To foster local economic development –LRGs are also closer to local economic and social actors than any other tier of governance and, as such, are best placed to formulate development strategies tailored to meet the needs of their territories and communities.

These needs include providing: an appropriately skilled and resourced public administration; effective support for local businesses and investors; and the political tools needed to deliver growth and innovation. They can be met by working in collaboration with all the relevant actors. They can also facilitate partnerships and mobilization by working closely with economic institutions (such as chambers of industry and commerce), small and medium-sized enterprises (SMEs), universities, research centres, trade unions and other representatives of civic society. Such coalitions have made crucial contributions to the creation of tailor-made policies and instruments that foster development-oriented policies that promote entrepreneurship and the creation of decent employment (SDG 8.3), as well as endogenous and inclusive sustainable development (SDG 8.4).

Drivers of Transformational Change for Localizing the SDGs

1. Sensitization and Engagement of Local Actors: It is widely acknowledged that good governance processes need to be inclusive and participatory. To engage meaningfully, people need to know about Agenda 2030, and local actors (including

civil society, private sector, and elected local councils) need to be engaged and play their role in implementation.

2. Accountability mechanisms: Accountable and participatory governance which underpins the SDGs is explicitly stated in Goal 16 on building peaceful, just and inclusive societies. It not only requires the presence of transparent and more inclusive institutions, it also requires a strong commitment to curb all forms of corruption, down to the local level.

3. Participatory planning and service delivery: Localization of Global and National development objectives is not a new process. The importance of inclusive planning and monitoring processes particularly at the local level cannot be underlined enough. Progress towards the SDGs must draw on the actions of local governments and galvanize participation from all actors in society.

4. Local economic development (LED): Our Global goals will not be reached unless our communities at the local level see concrete dividends.

5. Partnerships and the commitment to collective action: More than ever, we need to bring together National and local governments, the private sector, civil society and non-traditional players in the development arena such as foundations, social enterprises, traditional leaders, religious organizations and academia.

Government and Decision-Making Processes –Citizenship

- To what extent are the rights of citizenship enjoyed by women, men, all ages, and members of social groups?

- Are there any groups who do not (or cannot) register births?

- Are some groups excluded or disadvantaged from accessing

official information and processes?

- Do people living in urban slums enjoy equal rights by law and practice? Voice and accountability

- How is citizen voice and ability to hold public bodies to account affected by social identity?

- Formal political systems

- How inclusive and accessible are registration and voting procedures for citizens?

- What role do women play in formal decision-making processes at National, subNational, community, and household levels? Are other groups represented fairly?

- Do women and excluded groups occupy leadership positions in local, city, or country governance structures?

- Policy

- Is the government designing and implementing policies that meet the rights, needs, interests of all social groups (are there specific plans or programs in place for women and/or marginalized groups)?

Public Services

- To what extent are public services (health, Education, social protection, infrastructure, justice, security) being delivered (and perceived to be) accessible to women and men, and all social groups? What are the barriers?

- Are public goods and services provided in ways that reduce discrimination and allow all citizens to benefit?

- Who and where are the key gatekeepers to services? Whose, or what, interests do they serve?

- To what extent do official procedures discriminate against any social groups?

- To what extent is employment in public sector positions at different levels representative of the population including women and vulnerable and/or marginalized groups? Legal framework

- What International human rights conventions have been signed, ratified, or implemented in legislation?

- What legislation exists on violence against women and is it implemented?

- What is the role of traditional local, religious, and community governance and law?

- How equal, secure, and affordable access to justice for people of different ages, genders, and social identities?

- How does legislation and its implementation affect women's and girls' ownership of land and property, inheritance, and sexual and reproductive health and rights?

- Politics is gender discrimination recognized and discussed in National and local political?

- What other forms of discrimination are recognized in National and local politics?

- Who are the main political champions and opponents of gender equality and social inclusion?

Social – Vulnerability

- Which groups of women are poor and among the poorest?

- Which social groups are vulnerable or marginalized and why (e.g., persons with disabilities, ethnic, religious, occupational, socioeconomic status, etc.)?

- Which of these categories of people are the most marginalized, excluded, or vulnerable? Consider intersectional approaches or multiple marginalization of certain groups (e.g., women with disabilities, single and elderly women).

- Are there any groups of people who are described in local languages in very negative or derogatory ways? If yes, which ones? In what ways are they vulnerable, marginalized, or excluded?

- What is the status of migrants and refugees?

- Are those excluded and the poorest residents concentrated in particular locations (e.g., urban slums, outskirts of the city, etc.)?

- How is Climate Change and its impacts contributing to vulnerability and inequality? Are some groups more vulnerable than others?

- Who are the relevant stakeholders or people who influence the exclusion of marginalized or vulnerable groups?

- What will be the risk of excluding those marginalized and vulnerable in the project?

- Household and/or community relations

- What are the dominant social norms about men and women's roles and responsibilities?

- How does gender shape the household division of labor?

- How does household decision-making impact access to services and use of resources?

- How do age and disability affect intra-household relations? Social and cultural practices

- How are practices and institutions, such as those listed in the following brackets, related to gender inequality and social exclusion (kinship systems, inheritance, marriage practices, child-rearing practices, initiation, customary law, migrations, etc.)?

- Which social norms and/or cultural practices exist in this area that may prevent some people from benefiting from the project?

- How do those influential stakeholders or people, groups, or institutions reinforce the social and gender norms that impede social inclusion?

Civil Society, Media, and Technology

- What are the issues around which social groups mobilize?

- How extensive is participation by women and different social groups in voluntary organizations, political parties, or religious groups?

- Does civil society reach and/or represent people living in urban slums?

- Is there a disability movement?

- Are men involved in action on gender issues?

- Do women and vulnerable groups experience a digital divide?

What is the Level of Access of Women and Vulnerable Groups to Technology? Social Cohesion, Violence, and Conflict

- Which risks and instances of violence and tension are linked to social exclusion?

- What types of insecurity are prevalent (e.g., gang violence, gender-based violence, violent slum areas, trafficking of women, risk of increasing sexual exploitation, abuse and harassment)?

Economic – Income and Employment

- What is the relationship between gender, age, and different social identities and:

- labor markets and access to land and ownership?

- opportunities and barriers to earning income or participating in the labor market?

- distribution of income and wage gaps?

- access to employment and types of employment (whether formal or informal sectors)?

- wages and benefits?

- How do gender and social identity affect access to finance and key services?

- How are different social groups affected by the investment in climate and regulation, such as:

- access to business services?

- entrepreneurs, and opportunities or barriers to trading and selling products and services?

- Are business and employment markets segregated by social groups, gender, and formality?

- How does geography interact with identity in relation to access to income and employment (e.g., does living in a slum create inaccessibility, or cause discrimination)? Assets

- What is known about the distribution of wealth, land, property, and assets by gender and social group?

- How does gender and social identity shape urban land and housing tenure, access, control and use?

Advocacy

5 Key Elements of Advocacy:

- Networking: joining forces

- Knowledge and data: Building evidence

- Communication: Making evidence visible

- Multi-level governance: Building alliances with other levels of government

- Transparency and accountability: Building alliances with stakeholders What are the responsibilities of the related stakeholders?

Local and Regional Governments

- Establish priorities relating to the 17 SDGs based on local contexts.

- Identify and build on synergies and links with National SDG strategies.

- Identify synergies and links within local or regional administrations.

- Identify the actions and resources needed to implement priority areas.

- Draft an ad-hoc SDG-based plan.

- Set up local institutional arrangements and governance frameworks.

- Involve all local stakeholders in implementation to promote ownership.

Local and Regional Government Association Networks

- Support LRGs to improve their human, technical, and financial resources.

- Promote the exchange of best practices among their members.

- Promote decentralized cooperation.

- Promote the effective and full implementation of commitments to decentralization.

- Establish linkage with key Sectoral ministries and the ministry of local government for localization.

Monitoring

How can local and regional governments localize SDG monitoring?

1. Develop a set of localized indicators specific to each territory

2. Ensure that the information gathered by the LRGs is used in National SDG monitoring and reporting

3. Enable the participation of LRGs and stakeholders in the review of National plans

4. Use SDG indicators to monitor and assess local or regional plans

5. Ensure that local achievements are recognized and part of the National SDG progress reports

6. Promote the participation of LRGs in National monitoring

7. Collect data and monitor the progress at the subnational level

8. Adapt National indicators to local and regional context What are the responsibilities of the related stakeholders?

Local and Regional Governments Local and Regional Government Association Networks

- Collect, monitor, and analyze data at subnational level.

- Develop a set of localized indicators, specific to their territory.

- Participate in the monitoring and evaluation of the SDGs at the National level.

- Promote the participation of other stakeholders and ensure that the information gathered at the local level is used in National SDG monitoring and reporting.

- Promote the participation of LRGs and other stakeholders in the monitoring and evaluation of the SDGs at National level.

- Support LRGs in data collection, monitoring and assessment at local level.

Creating an Enabling Environment for the Implementation of the SDGs

The active engagement of LRGs should be based on the 4Cs approach to ensure an effective and accountable systemic approach to achieve the SDGs and its targets.

The 4Cs approach consists of:

1. COHERENCE of policies across National Sectoral policies. Across different themes and ministries, the ultimate goal for sustainable development should encompass coherent efforts, also keeping in mind the balance of the economic, environmental and social dimensions;

2. COHESION of National and subnational plans and strategies, paying the necessary attention to specific needs of subnational regions, particularly those that lag behind, in order to ensure more integrated and balanced regional growth and social

cohesion;

3. COORDINATION between National and subnational level to align strategies and ensure the necessary support to action at the subnational level. Mechanisms for multi-level governance also need to be considered for coordination among regional and local governments;

4. COOPERATION among all levels of government and with all stakeholders will be key to the success of the 2030 Agenda. Establishing partnerships and involving civil-society, business, academia and local communities should be at the heart of the implementation efforts of LRGs.

LRGs find themselves at different stages of the SDG implementation process.

PREPARATION

National Level

- Preparing National strategies (integration/alignment of the SDGs within National development strategies (NDSs) or development of a 2030 Agenda plan).

- Appointing a responsible National coordination body and building an inclusive governance arrangement to promote a 'whole-of-government' and a 'whole-of-society' approach to SDG implementation.

- Formulating National monitoring and evaluation framework and indicators.

- Providing information and consultation (National and local).

- Establishing localization strategies for SDG implementation by vertically and horizontally aligning policies.

- Instituting dedicated means of implementation through

technical assistance and training programmers and financing mechanisms.

- Introducing a National reporting system for the preparation of the VNR with a multi-stakeholder participatory approach.

Local/Regional Level

- Aligning local development plans (LDPs) with the SDGs and/or National development plans (NDPs) that already have integrated within the SDGs.

- Establishing local/regional coordination bodies by building governance arrangements.

- Strengthening local information and consultation.

- Setting priorities and targets to implement local 2030 Agenda plans.

Form of Integrated Local Governance

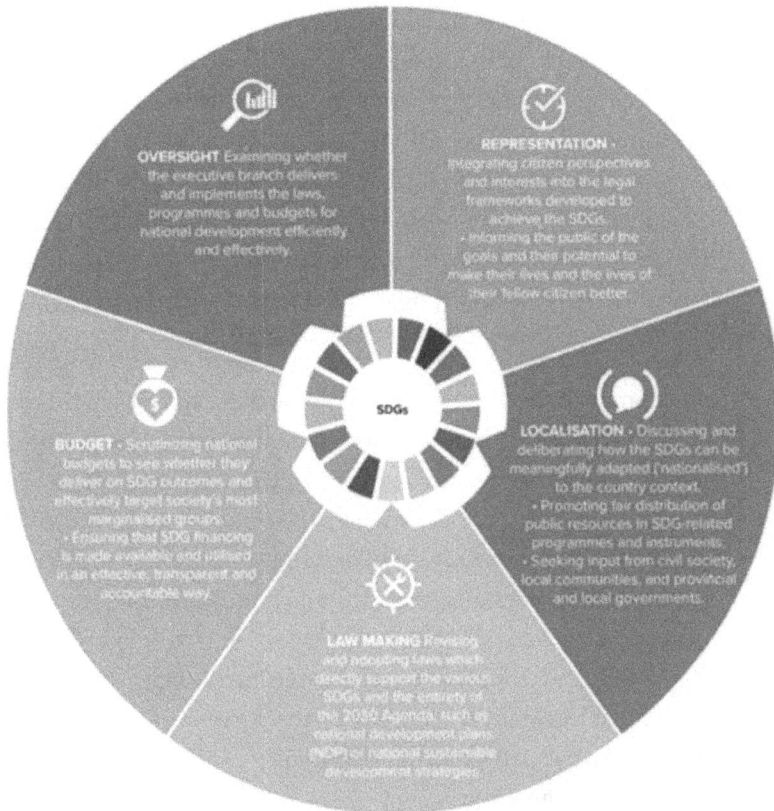

OVERSIGHT. Examining whether the executive branch delivers and implements the laws, programmes and budgets for national development efficiently and effectively.

REPRESENTATION. Integrating citizen perspectives and interests into the legal frameworks developed to achieve the SDGs. • Informing the public of the goals and their potential to make their lives and the lives of their fellow citizen better.

BUDGET. Scrutinizing national budgets to see whether they deliver on SDG outcomes and effectively target society's most marginalised groups. • Ensuring that SDG financing is made available and utilised in an effective, transparent and accountable way.

LOCALISATION. Discussing and deliberating how the SDGs can be meaningfully adapted ('nationalised') to the country context. • Promoting fair distribution of public resources in SDG-related programmes and instruments. • Seeking input from civil society, local communities, and provincial and local governments.

LAW MAKING. Revising and adopting laws which directly support the various SDGs and the entirety of the 2030 Agenda, such as national development plans (NDP) or national sustainable development strategies.

SDGs

Integration between the policies, priorities, and programs of different government bodies is essential for balanced SDG implementation, both at the local and National levels. Forms of integrated local governance include:

Forms of Integrated Local Governance Include:

1. Territorial coordination between local governments: SDG 11 promotes a place-based approach to development. This must be supported through mechanisms of territorial integration; of policy, planning, infrastructure, and accountability across

neighboring administrative borders. Be it through formal structures of regional or metropolitan governance, or informal cooperation between municipalities, territorial strategies aim to improve development linkages within the region to reduce territorial inequalities, protect ecological systems, and improve economic productivity in the region as a whole. Resultant outcomes from territorial coordination may include integrated transportation networks, regionally-coordinated service delivery, controlled urban growth and protection of agricultural lands, and stronger labor market linkages.

2. Horizontal coordination across departments/ministries: Horizontal integration refers to coordinated policy-making across different sectors of government to optimize resource utilization and aim for mutually beneficial outcomes. There is a need for governments to re-evaluate sector-based governance, establish cooperation mechanisms between different departments, and embed cross-cutting issues like environmental protection, gender, economic inclusion, and Climate Change adaptation and mitigation into government-wide operations. Horizontal integration is critical to the success of the SDGs in order to balance social, economic, and environmental development outcomes.

3. Vertical coordination with National and state/regional governments: Local governments can work more closely with higher levels of government to jointly address development, and for better-coordinated approaches to planning, implementation, and reporting. Vertical coordination in SDG governance will promote improved resource allocation based on knowledge of local needs and development gaps.

Inter-Municipal or Territorial Coordination

- Inter-municipal agencies: Formal or informal arrangements of cooperation among the municipal organizations within an identified or implied metropolitan region, for policy decisions that have spillover effects beyond administrative borders.

- Sectoral governance boards: Executive boards that amalgamate service delivery across municipal borders, for greater efficiency and fairer distribution of costs and resources. This may be for services such as waste management, fire protection, water supply and sanitation, energy, roads, etc.

- Metropolitan governments: Formalized, legal institutions that form an intermediate level of governance in complex metropolitan regions that comprise a large number of local governments.

Inter-Departmental or Horizontal Coordination

- Inter-departmental agencies: May be formed through informal cooperation or local government directives. Inter-departmental agencies are more effective when formed around multi-sector development projects.

- Cross-Sectoral departments: The Department of Planning, Department of Statistics, or other appropriate cross-Sectoral institution may be assigned the additional responsibility of identifying and facilitating multi-Sectoral cooperation and action for sustainable development.

- Digital Platforms: Shared digital platforms (possibly GIS-based) that are accessible to all departments, fostering a culture of data and information sharing that empowers Sectoral departments to take more informed decisions within the larger framework of local government.

Vertical Coordination Between Multiple Levels of Government

- Parastatal agencies: Representative institutions of higher levels of government that work in the local or regional sphere, often in an executive capacity. While the risk of parastatal agencies replacing local governments exists, they also have the potential to work with local governments, for greater capacity development and closer cooperation between levels of government.

- Vertical funds: Vertical funds link high level policies with the capacity for implementation at local levels, providing ear-marked funding for programmatic planning, and delivery of policy outcomes.

- Special Purpose Vehicles: Special Purpose Vehicles are partnerships formed for joint planning and implementation of specific projects, in which National or regional governments may provide access to long-term finance lending, and retaining oversight of project management, facilitated and/or implemented by local governments (with or without the help of private agencies).

- Accountability mechanisms: Through periodic audits or M&E frameworks, multi-level accountability mechanisms can be closely linked with financial allocation decisions for greater efficacy and to better match local needs with resource flows and institutional capacity and mandates.

Inter-Departmental Agencies -

May be formed through informal cooperation or local government directives. Inter-departmental agencies are more effective when formed around multi-sector development projects.

Cross-Sectoral Departments –

The Department of Planning, Department of Statistics, or other appropriate cross-Sectoral institution may be assigned the additional responsibility of identifying and facilitating multi-Sectoral cooperation and action for sustainable development.

Digital Platforms –

Shared digital platforms (possibly GIS-based) that are accessible to all departments, fostering a culture of data and information sharing that empowers Sectoral departments to take more informed decisions within the larger framework of local government.

- What are then the new strategies to support local governance?

- Taking fully into account the local cultural and institutional context: All interventions are carried out in a specific context that greatly affects their impact. There are many institutional actors involved and numerous issues to be taken into account. It suggests (a) that sufficient resources should be deployed to ensure adequate prior knowledge of the context, and (b) that, as a corollary, key aspects of the local context should be taken into account in formulating the action strategy.

- Increasing levels of participation: the level of information-sharing increases local participation and a degree of consultation and contestability arises from increased levels of local participation in decision-making.

- Adapt support for local governance to National strategy: Local development cannot be divorced from its regional and National context. It is therefore important to link with National authorities and take fully into account the National strategy when designing measures in support of local governance.

Such an embedded approach has at least three advantages:

- It makes it easier for de-concentrated state agencies to provide technical support to local authorities,

- It encourages synergy between local-authority development policies and sector-wide policies formulated and implemented by central government, and

- It encourages local and National authorities to capitalise on, and share, relevant experiences.

- Enhance negotiation and consultation between actors: Negotiation and regular consultation between actors is critical to the success of support for local governance, as it enables the actors to agree both on the goals and on the ways and means of attaining them. It may also help strengthen actors' organizational and institutional capacities and hence their capacity to monitor and evaluate support for local governance.

- Encourage transparency and accountability: Many different actors are involved in local governance, some of whom pursue different goals. It is important, in the interests of all concerned, to cultivate a sense of responsibility among them all. Creating mechanisms that make those in charge more accountable for what they do and that enable the public to obtain clear information from them may make it easier to follow up on actions taken by local actors.

What is the Connection between Decentralization and Local Governance Approach?

The concepts of local governance and decentralization, at times used interchangeably, are related but different concepts. Decentralization is primarily a National political, legislative, institutional and fiscal process. While local governance can be affected by decentralization processes - for example, if local governments are expected to provide services formerly offered through National organizations - it may or may or may not be accompanied by decentralization, representative or participatory democratic processes, transparency, accountability or other defining characteristics of 'good' local governance.

Decentralization directly influences local governance by setting up a new layer of political and economic power.

Decentralization opens new spaces where the management of local power can be examined and questioned. It opens new challenges

1. Population: Decentralization creates new local powers, in addition to those that already exist (customary powers, religion, police, tax collectors…)

2. Local elites: Decentralization creates new elites and power holders

3. Administration: Decentralization means losing part of their power

4. NGOs in service delivery: Local governments are now the legitimate actors, competition for resources

5. Economic agents, private sectors: Decentralization multiplies the actors to be taken into account in procurement

The Sources of Potential Conflicts are Manifold

- Local elections are the key to legitimacy of local governments. Yet such elections are not a self-evident exercise in countries with a fragile or emerging democratic culture. Furthermore, newly elected local bodies must find their place and earn their legitimacy alongside existing forms of authority.

- Effective local governments are seldom created from the top. It is dangerous to assume that local governments can be created by a few central decisions to transfer functions and authority over resources - and that municipalities should just wait for this to happen. Historically local government has tended to develop as those in the localities have taken action to demonstrate their determination and ability to set their own priorities. This implies a tradition or acceptance of challenging the centre – a set of conditions that are often lacking.

- Decentralization implies an overall rethinking of inter-governmental relations and new demarcation lines with regard to roles and responsibilities between the different layers of government. One of the most important lessons of successful decentralization programmers is that democratic decentralization (devolution) involves a redefinition of central and local government tasks and resources. This cannot be achieved without effective intergovernmental relations. Yet this is particularly challenging in countries where decentralization is seen as a 'zero-sum' power game in which the centre stands to lose rather than as a 'positive-sum' power game in which all players win over time.

- Decentralization fundamentally affects the "accountability chain" in development processes. This includes checking 'where the money goes' that is channeled to the local level. Does it really reach the ultimate beneficiaries? Public expenditure tracking surveys can be a most useful tool to monitor budget execution.

- Decentralization involves building an active citizenship. The process of decentralization responds to the aspiration to have a greater say in the management of local affairs. This often requires a 'bottom-up' struggle

  a. To alter existing power relations;

  b. To get rid of the habit to use local governments as a mechanism for gathering votes;

    c. To empower communities; and

    d. To construct and nurture citizenship.

- Highly centralized governments are likely to resist the emergence of citizen movements claiming for genuine democratic space at local level.

- Competition for donor funding.

- Donor choices of geographic focus, partners and institutional 'entry points may introduce biases or tilt power structures in favor of one actor or another. Competition is likely to increase as local governments gain momentum and credibility. This tension is already noticeable between local governments and non-governmental organizations in the search for local development funds. Increasingly competition also takes place between central and local governments (e.g. for Sectoral funds).

Political Decentralization

- Assessing current, and identifying potential, resources;

- Clarifying the fiscal responsibilities and obligations of local governments;

- Improving the management of transfers from the central government and improving the management of internally generated resources;

- Optimizing revenue collection methods and processes;

- Allocating resources among different levels and/or sectors of local development;

- Developing appropriate accounting systems;

- Designing information, management and auditing systems;

- Training managers and leaders

Fiscal Decentralization

This figure describes the various key 'ingredients' that need be considered in designing a fiscal decentralization system involving several levels of government. Among these aspects, the likely impact of fiscal decentralization is particularly important. It invites policymakers to focus on policy areas such as (1) economic efficiency, (2) macroeconomic stability, (3) income redistribution (inter-regional or interpersonal equity) and (4) political efficiency.

Administrative Decentralization

There are three major forms of administrative decentralization: decentralization, delegation, and devolution.

Why Assess Local Governance?

The purpose for undertaking an assessment of local governance is of utmost importance as it is the purpose that decides the scope of the assessment, the methodology and the indicators to be applied, and not vice versa. Conducting an assessment with vague objectives fails to provide proper development outcomes and can be a waste of time and resources.

The rationale for assessing decentralization and local governance is as follows: What are the general principles of local governance?

Democracy and Legitimacy

- The people of the country can exercise power directly (citizens can run for office and get elected) and indirectly through the local government bodies (when citizens by the means of elections appoint governing bodies);

- Local government bodies and their officials must act within the boundaries of their authority and by the means outlined by the law.

Transparency and Openness

- In a democratic society government must be not only effective, but transparent as well;

- Every member of the community is entitled to know what actions the government takes.

- Operate in the state of openness to its citizens

Collective Nature

- The majority of decisions of local government agencies are not made by one official, but by a group, which is a more accurate way to express public opinion;

- Collective decision-making prevents usurpation of power by one individual;

- There is an established quorum necessary for a representative body to function and a quorum necessary for adopting decisions.

Appointment by Election

- The community independently appoints local government bodies by election;

- The opinion of the community about who should hold office does not depend on the National policy;

- It is the direct way to exercise democracy on the given territory.

Legislative Autonomy

- Local government bodies must have their own functions and responsibilities outlined in the state law;

- Local government bodies are legal entities that act independently within their authority and that are accountable for their actions in compliance with the law;

- Local government bodies must have complete authority and exclusive rights not shared with other bodies to implement their initiatives concerning any issues falling within the jurisdiction of local government.

Organizational Autonomy

- The main subjects of local government - its communities and bodies - are not a part of the state apparatus;

- Communities and their government agencies must have a capacity to determine their own structure that takes into account local factors and can provide effective administration and management;

- When acting within the law, local government agencies are not subordinate to other authorities, and any kind of administrative control of their actions is possible only in order to secure compliance with laws;

- Actions of local government bodies and officials can be monitored by the state only under the law, and this should not lead to the interference of state bodies and officials in the issues within the authority of local government.

Financial Autonomy

- A community and its local government bodies have the right to possess, use, and dispose of communal property as well as communal funds, sufficient for a local government to perform its functions;

- The economic and financial base of local government consists of movable and immovable assets, local budget revenues, and other assets, such as land and natural resources within the communal property;

- Communal ownership is an independent from state form of public ownership;

- Local budgets are independent and are not included in the National budget.

State Support and Guarantees for LG

- National government supports local governments via partial funding on condition of compliance with the regulations concerning the administration of local governance, such as self-organization and self-responsibility;

- A democratic state politically supports local government by creating constitutional, administrative, legal, economic and financial guarantees for its effective operation.

Accountability & Responsibility of LG Bodies and Officials to Communities

- Local government bodies and officials are held accountable for breaking the state law

- Government bodies and officials report on their actions to their constituents;

- In the case that a local government violates the law and interests of the community, its bodies can be terminated early.

Judicial Protection of the Rights of LG

- Communities and local government bodies have a right to appeal to a court in order to protect their rights and interests judicially;

- When prescribed by law, state bodies can also represent rights and interests of communities and local government bodies.

Balancing Local and State Interests

- The purview of local government consists of issues that represent the needs of the community;

- In its actions, a local government must balance communal and state interests. For example, it must exercise efficiently and responsibly certain functions of state government bodies if such authority is delegated to it by the law;

- The state may entrust local government bodies with certain responsibilities of the executive branch of the government, and the local government has to administer those responsibilities;

- When local government bodies administer their own responsibilities, they act independently and comply only with the law. However, when they administer delegated responsibilities, they are under the control of corresponding state bodies.

Subsidiarity

- Functions of local governance must be performed primarily by those bodies, that are the closest to citizens;

- When entrusting a local government body with one or another function, it is necessary to take into account the volume and type of tasks, and also the requirements of "efficiency and cost-effectiveness";

- The division of responsibilities between various levels of local government must be organized in such a manner as to both bring the decision-making process as close to citizens as possible and to ensure that these levels of local government possess all the necessary organizational, material and financial resources.

Ubiquity

- Local governance must be exercised throughout the entire territory of the country, which means there are no territories that are not under the jurisdiction of a community and a local government.

In terms of measuring local governance, there are four broad focus areas which an assessment might address: local governance, decentralization processes; local democracy, and local government.

However, some challenges are expected throughout the way. What are the challenges of financing for sustainable development?

At the National Level

1. The UN estimates the gap in financing to achieve the Sustainable Development Goals (SDGs) at $2.5 trillion per year in developing countries alone (UNCTAD, 2014).

2. Global financial assets are sufficient to meet the financing needs of the 2030 Development Agenda, but the challenge is how to channel them into SDG sectors, enhance the risk-return profiles of new and sometimes vulnerable investments, and generate sustained impact on the ground. Channeling available finance towards the SDGs and the goals of the Paris Agreement are constrained by a range of challenges.

3. Another dilemma is the apparent conflict between the particularly acute funding needs in structurally weak economies, especially LDCs, necessitating a significant increase in private sector investment, and the fact that especially these countries face the greatest difficulty in attracting such investment. Without targeted policy intervention and support measures there is a real risk that investors will continue to see operating conditions and risks in LDCs as prohibitive.

4. Beneath the Global headline figures, economic progress remains highly uneven across regions and countries. In most parts of East and South Asia, economic activity continues to grow rapidly, underpinned by robust domestic demand and macroeconomic policy support.

5. Growing Financial Risks: Short-term financial market volatility has increased due to COVID-19. Prior to that, an extended period of low interest rates had incentivized riskier behaviour throughout the financial system.

6. High Debt Risk: Debt risks will likely rise further in the most vulnerable countries. 44% of least developed and other low-income developing countries are currently at high risk or in debt distress.

7. Increasing Trade Restrictions: Substantial new trade restrictions have been introduced: the trade coverage of import-restrictive measures are almost 10 times larger than two years prior.

8. Increasing Environmental Shocks: Greenhouse gas emissions continue to rise, posing risks to sustainable development. Between 2014–2018, the estimated number of weather-related loss events worldwide increased by over 30 per cent compared to the preceding five years.

At the Local Level

One of the biggest hurdles facing local governments today is the mismatch between their increasing responsibilities and static revenues.

Weak local finances may be the result of various factors, including:

1. National government restrictions on local powers of revenue generation;

2. Limited local capacity to collect revenues and/or deliver services;

3. Local revenue generation disincentives from poorly designed fiscal transfer programs;

4. Inadequate funding as a result of inadequate financial planning;

5. Low political credibility/accountability of local governments, weakening revenue compliance; and

6. Climate Change requires resilient planning and infrastructure.

Chapter 5 - Strategies for Closing the Green Finance Gap

Climate Finance

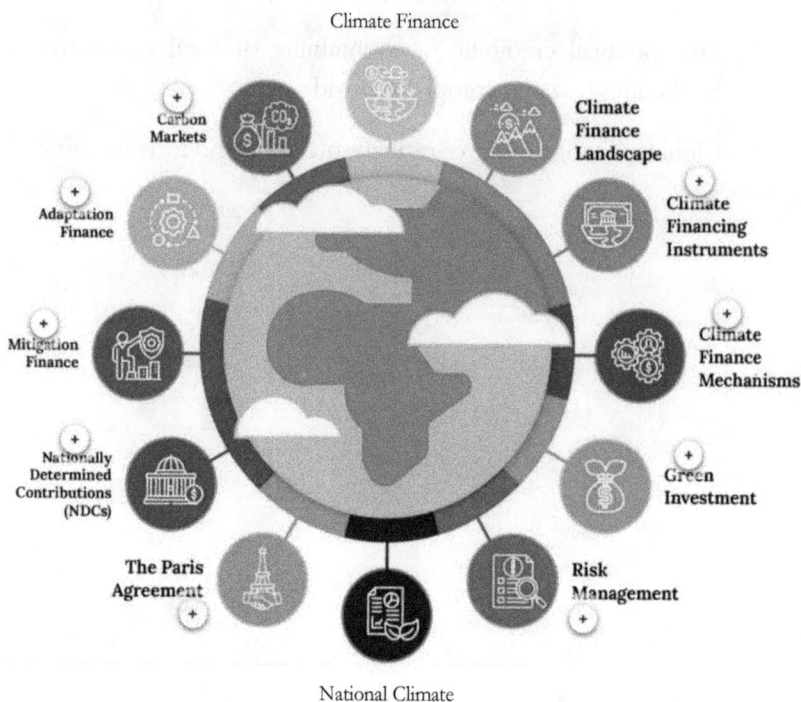

National Climate

Narrowing the green finance gap necessitates a comprehensive strategy that combines initiatives from both public and private actors.

- **Policy Instruments**

  Governments have a key role to play in attracting private capital towards green projects. One approach involves implementing policies like carbon pricing, which essentially puts a cost on emitting greenhouse gases. This incentivizes businesses and individuals to shift towards cleaner alternatives. The European Union's success with tax breaks for renewable energy and energy efficiency demonstrates the effectiveness of this strategy in stimulating billions of euros in green investments. Furthermore, establishing clear and consistent green taxonomies – classification systems for environmentally friendly activities – alongside mandatory environmental disclosure standards can significantly improve transparency. This reduces the perceived risk for private investors, making green projects more attractive.

- **De-risking Strategies**

  Public and private collaboration is crucial for mobilizing significant green finance. Public-private partnerships (PPPs) offer a win-win solution. By sharing risks, these partnerships allow governments to leverage their funds to attract private investment. A prime example is the IFC's (International Finance Corporation) successful partnership with private investors to develop a massive USD 1.1 billion wind and solar farm project in Egypt. Furthermore, development finance institutions and multilateral banks can play a vital role by offering guarantees and other risk mitigation instruments. These instruments essentially act as safety nets for private investors, making green projects more appealing despite potential uncertainties.

- **Financial Innovation**

  Financial innovation is key to unlocking new green investment opportunities. Green bonds, for example, have exploded in popularity, reaching a staggering USD 2 trillion in 2022 as reported by OECD. This reflects the growing investor interest in environmentally conscious projects.

  Additionally, blended finance structures, which combine public and private funds, offer a promising solution. The Climate Investment Funds (CIF) successfully use this approach to unlock financing for crucial climate-resilient infrastructure projects in developing countries.

- **Capacity Building**

  Capacity-building programs can equip these countries with the skills needed to design, develop, and present bankable green projects, making them more attractive to investors. On the other hand, supporting green financial literacy initiatives can increase investor confidence by improving their understanding of green investment opportunities and the associated risks and rewards. This two-pronged approach fosters a more informed and engaged environment, where developing nations can present compelling green projects and investors can make informed decisions to support a sustainable future.

- **Technological Advancements**

  Technological advancements hold immense potential to bridge the green finance gap. Increased investment in clean technologies, like renewable energy, can make them more cost-competitive. This not only attracts private capital but also accelerates innovation, further driving down costs. The International Renewable Energy Agency (IRENA) estimates an annual investment of USD 1.3 trillion in renewables by 2030 is needed to achieve climate goals. By making clean technologies more attractive and affordable through innovation, technological advancements can play a critical role in unlocking the vast private capital needed to achieve our climate goals.

The Path to a Greener Future

Bridging the green finance gap is not an insurmountable challenge. By collaborating, harnessing innovation, and creating an enabling environment, public and private actors can mobilize the necessary resources to fuel the transition towards a sustainable future. While the gap seems sizable, several encouraging trends offer hope:

- Growing Investor Interest: Awareness of environmental, social, and governance (ESG) factors is rising among investors, leading to increased interest in green investments.

- Policy Action: Governments around the world are implementing policies and regulations to promote green finance.

- Technological Progress: The cost of renewable energy technologies is falling rapidly, making them more attractive investment options.

Closing the green finance gap is not just about mobilizing capital, it is about transforming our economic and financial systems to prioritize sustainability. By closing this gap, we can unlock a future powered by clean energy, resilient infrastructure, and sustainable growth for all. The time to invest in a greener future is now.

We should think of the range of financial sources as a staircase: steps which build on each other to add up to $1.3 trillion. Here's what each step represents—and the challenges to surmount at each level.

Drive urgent climate action on the following key issues:

- Scale-up climate finance: Government should Work to identify novel mechanisms and funding sources to support the $1.3 trillion agreed for climate mitigation and adaptation in developing countries.

- Strengthen National and regional climate action: Mobilise National and regional networks to support ambitious, actionable, and integrate NDCs and their implementation.

- Conserve and advance sustainable development in tropical forests: Advocate for science and evidence-based solutions, engaging Indigenous peoples and local communities for conservation and sustainable development across the tropical forest regions of the Country.

- Accelerate a just energy transition: Advance the UN Secretary-General's goal to triple renewable energy capacity and double energy efficiency by encouraging multinational cooperation.

First Step: Public Climate Finance

Figure1 - Government Bodies and Processes that Constitute a CCFF

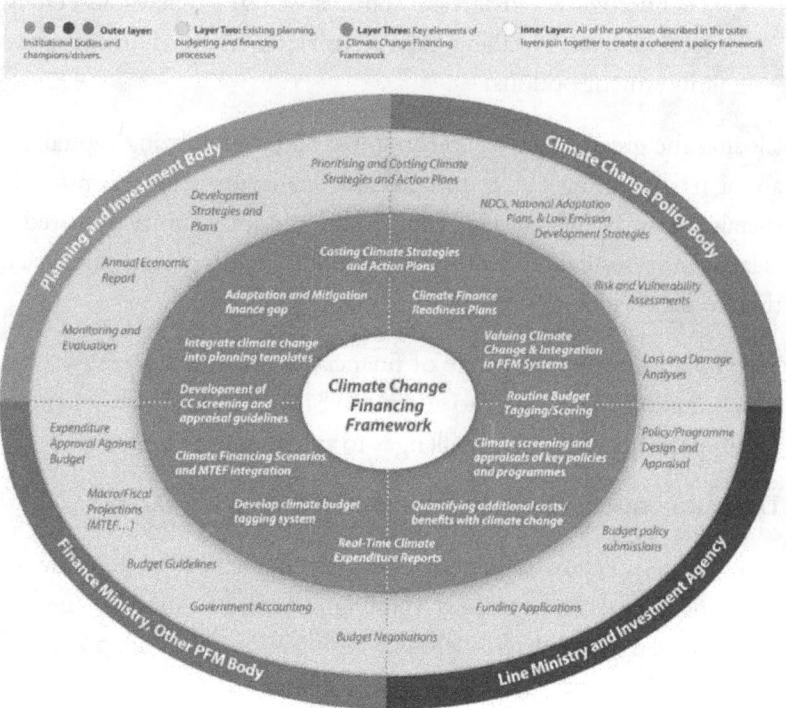

Note that the diagram above represents a stylised/suggested model and is not proscriptive. Different countries will have different models according to their institutional arrangements.

The first and largest step in the staircase is money that is provided by governments from rich, historically responsible countries to support the climate action efforts of the poorest countries. This is the basis of the current $100 billion goal that was agreed on in Copenhagen and was first met in 2022, two years past the deadline. Everyone agrees it needs to be increased—but by how much?

Some rich countries have argued that this step should amount to about $250 billion per year. They describe this money as "mobilised," rather than "provided." In other words, "mobilised" finance includes assumptions that the investment is pulled through from the private sector, rather than being money provided directly from National coffers.

Developing countries, meanwhile, think that this step should be a little bigger— around $300 billion. This needs to be public money, they argue: it should be made up of grants that are easy to access and do not create more debt. It should be deployable in line with the National plans of the countries that receive it.

Second Step: Diversification of Sources

Some countries say that the definition of which countries count as developed—aka, which nations should contribute to that "mobilised' first financing step—needs to be updated. The definition, which dates back to the Kyoto protocol in 1994, does not include countries like China, now the world's second-largest economy, and Saudi Arabia, a G20 state.

In Baku this year, for the first time in a COP setting, China has described its support to developing countries as "climate finance,"—a nod to the request to be part of this effort. China has pointed to its current efforts totalling about 3.1 billion—depending on how you define it, it could be a lot more. But China has also made it very clear that this contribution is voluntary. The "first step" money, by contrast, would be a firm commitment for which countries are accountable. Other countries, like Saudi Arabia, have historically held firm against being included as a donor country.

Third Step: Multilateral Development Banks

Big development banks, like the World Bank, believe they can deliver $120 billion a year by 2030 to low- and middle-income countries, including $42 billion for adaptation. When added with an anticipated $65 billion from the private sector, this is more than the 74.7 billion collective climate financing mobilised in 2023 for low- and middle-income countries. Still, the Independent High-Level Expert Group says banks must triple their financing by 2030 to support climate goals: $480 billion is possible without affecting their ratings.

The view that multilateral development banks are under-delivering on their potential is also the focus of the Bridgetown initiative led by Barbados PM Mia Mottley. If those recommendations were implemented, banks could further leverage their balance sheets and deploy in developing countries "special drawing rights" which have only been available to traditional donor countries. Multilateral development banks must also become more involved in the Global effort to develop solutions for relieving debt. For many developing economies, the burden of debt repayment as interest rates rise is far outstripping any of the income from climate finance; there is no formal forum or mechanism through which countries can seek to restructure their debt with creditors, whether "official" (governments, MDBs) or "commercial" (bondholders, commodities traders, banks). Preferential rates, debt brakes and debt forgiveness must be coordinated to ensure the benefits of climate finance aren't wiped out by the vagaries of the markets. While MDBs can play a crucial role, it's important to note that addressing Global debt will require help from all participants in this financial ladder.

Fourth Step: Innovative Sources of Finance

This step represents a diverse set of proposals; this step alone could probably be described as a series of steps or a flight. It includes:

- Global levy on stock-market trades of 0.1%, could raise up to $418 billion year

- Levy on shipping of $100 per ton of carbon dioxide emitted could raise $80

- A billion per year they write could be delivered by a G20 wealth tax proposal by economist Gabriel Zucman. $2 billion a year

- $80 billion a year come from voluntary carbon markets, says Mark Carney

- Global shipping emissions tax under discussion at the IMO$121 billion a year

- Amount a $9-a-flight 'frequent flying levy' could raise, proposed by ICCT $720 billion by 2030

- Climate damages tax on oil majors, backed by Greenpeace

These set of proposals stacks up to $1.6 trillion—but it's already 2025. The world is already late on delivering $1 trillion. Not one of these mechanisms is set up to deliver. What's more, the biggest vehicle in this list—the proposed oil major tax—would be implemented on companies that are generally either based in the US, which is about to leave the Paris Agreement, state-owned and therefore protected, and/or have the political links and lobbying and legal firepower to ensure it doesn't happen for a long time.

So how much can we depend on this step delivering? That picture will emerge over the coming years, because countries back different proposals based on their circumstances. But it is clear the potential is considerable.

Fifth Step: Private Finance

At the top of this ladder is private finance. The private sector holds the majority of the world's wealth—the sector manages more than $210 trillion in assets—yet it has invested comparatively little in climate finance.

Governments and public institutions have a pivotal role in creating the right conditions to mobilize and unlock private finance. Current estimates indicate that private sector mobilization could generate up to

$650 billion for climate action by 2035. Public leaders need to focus on creating the right conditions for private finance to mobilize on this issue.

Sixth step: National Adaptation Plans

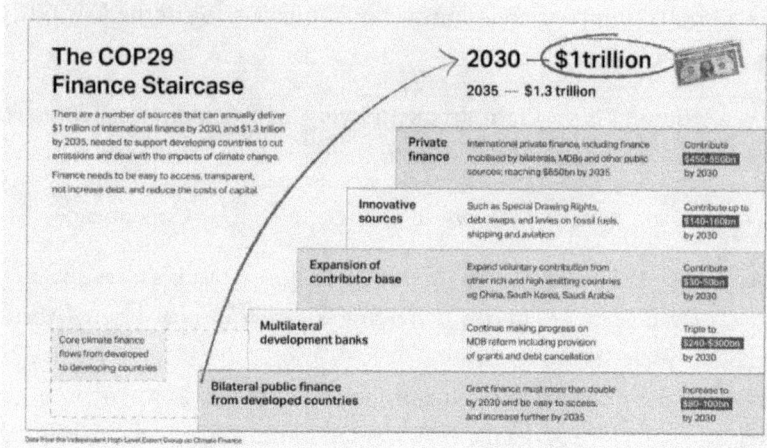

The COP29 Finance Staircase

2030 — $1 trillion
2035 — $1.3 trillion

There are a number of sources that can annually deliver $1 trillion of international finance by 2030, and $1.3 trillion by 2035, needed to support developing countries to cut emissions and deal with the impacts of climate change.

Finance needs to be easy to access, transparent, not increase debt, and reduce the costs of capital.

Private finance	International private finance, including finance mobilised by bilaterals, MDBs and other public sources; reaching $650bn by 2035.	Contribute $450-850bn by 2030
Innovative sources	Such as Special Drawing Rights, debt swaps, and levies on fossil fuels, shipping and aviation	Contribute up to $140-160bn by 2030
Expansion of contributor base	Expand voluntary contribution from other rich and high emitting countries eg China, South Korea, Saudi Arabia	Contribute $30-50bn by 2030
Multilateral development banks	Continue making progress on MDB reform including provision of grants and debt cancellation	Triple to $240-$300bn by 2030
Bilateral public finance from developed countries	Grant finance must more than double by 2030 and be easy to access, and increase further by 2035	Increase to $80-100bn by 2030

Core climate finance flows from developed to developing countries

Data from the Independent High Level Expert Group on Climate Finance

National plans to adapt to climate impacts and build resilience are no longer a "nice to have" for any country—developed or developing. They are absolutely crucial to protect human lives, health, jobs, supply chains and entire economies, and to enable low-inflation growth.

Deadly wildfires, devastating storms, droughts and floods hitting all countries provide irrefutable proof.

Between 1970 and 2021, extreme weather, climate and water-related events caused 11,778 reported disasters, leading to over 2 million deaths and US$ 4.3 trillion in economic losses (WMO).

Central to the solutions are National Adaptation Plans (NAPs), which must span all levels of government, engage leaders from diverse socio-political backgrounds, be investment-oriented and mobilize capital from public, private, domestic and International sources.

Building climate resilience is crucial to save lives, communities and economies, but much more than that – to transform them for the better.

Climate adaptation refers to preparing for and responding to the current and anticipated effects of Climate Change. It involves modifying processes, practices, and structures to minimize potential damages or capitalize on opportunities linked to Climate Change.

The climate adaptation market is experiencing significant growth due to increasing awareness of Climate Change impacts, more frequent and severe weather events, and rising economic losses from climate-related disasters. Governments and private sectors are recognizing the necessity of adaptation strategies, further driving investments and the development of new technologies aimed at mitigating climate risks and enhancing resilience.

Long-Term Resilience: Climate adaptation for sustainability focuses on building long-term resilience in communities, ecosystems, and economies to withstand the impacts of Climate Change.

Sustainable Infrastructure: Designing and upgrading infrastructure to be climate-resilient while using eco-friendly materials and reducing resource consumption (e.g., green buildings, flood-resistant infrastructure).

Adaptation for Economic Sustainability: Helping industries transition to sustainable practices that mitigate climate risks, ensuring economic stability and long-term growth.

Water and Resource Management: Developing sustainable water management systems to deal with water scarcity, and promoting efficient use of natural resources in agriculture, industry, and urban areas.

Development partners can do more to meet the scale of today's challenges while making the Global economic system more equitable and absorbent to shocks.

Three broad areas for targeted, risk-informed and resilient development Co-operation:

- Boosting social protection and investing in decent job creation. Building on lessons learnt from the COVID-19 crisis, and in anticipation of future crises and transitions, we must invest in universal social protection and decent job creation, which function both as critical shock absorbers and as enablers of inclusive growth. The UN Global Accelerator on Jobs and Social Protection for Just Transitions provides a coherent framework for short- and long-term actions and solutions.

- Strengthening climate adaptation. Development co-operation must do more to support the most vulnerable countries as they navigate the climate crisis. Building on the recent achievements of COP 27, especially on loss and damage, we must mainstream climate resilience into development co-operation and meet climate finance commitments while bringing climate and development finance closer together in recognition of the need to accelerate just transitions for all. Sub-Saharan Africa, for example, will need billions of dollars this decade to protect itself from climate-related disasters. In this regard, the Secretary-General will continue to advocate for a large-scale SDG Stimulus to mobilise the financing needed at scale for investments in long-term sustainable development.

- Harnessing digital transformations. The pandemic has accelerated the digital transformation through more effective digital learning platforms, strengthened e-commerce and e-procurement systems and other innovative digital technologies. We must support digital interventions Nationally and Globally, especially those that address multi-dimensional vulnerability and build resilience.

Build capacity of city officials to conduct vulnerability assessments and implement nature-based approaches to enhance climate resilience in cities. Focus on (1) Introduction to the Climate Hazard Vulnerability Assessment (CHVA) framework to prioritize resilience actions in cities, (2) Nature-based solutions to tackle extreme heat in cities, and (3) Nature-based solutions to mitigate urban flooding. City government officials from Global South cities, National government officials with urban development mandates should be trained.

Progress in four key areas is the key to climate action

- Responding to the UN's first Global Stocktake;

- Transforming Earth's systems — including energy, food land use, and cities;

- Building resilience to the increasingly severe impacts of Climate Change; and

- Delivering climate finance to the world's most vulnerable nations.

By Learning from examples, stories and journeys from people who have been working on these.

1. Re-calibrating our relationship with the Community of Life, Nature and Earth, our Home.

2. Rethinking our ethical responsibility with the well-being of future generations.

3. Rethinking Education for the current times, transformative learning, Education for sustainability and Global citizenship.

4. Exploring how The Earth Charter intersects with the SDGs, the Pact for the Future, and the aspiration of building an ecological civilization and the concept of Earth Trusteeship.

5. It's time to change the way we think about changing the world.

Later is too late.

The Pact for the Future, an outcome document of UN COP29 focused on key issues, including sustainable development and financing; peace and security; science and innovation; youth and future generations; and the reform of Global governance.

Monitor, learn and mobilise action towards the transformational shifts needed to protect both people and the planet.

Learn How - Global Snapshot of each shift

To limit warming to below 1.5 degrees C, halt biodiversity loss and secure a more just, equitable society, we need to transform 14 Global systems-70 critical changes– what we call shifts – that can help deliver systemwide transformations. These shifts are changes within a system, and when multiple shifts work together, they can spur transformational change.

No single technology, policy or actor alone can achieve these critical shifts. Rather, it will take a community of people working together across systems to employ innovative solutions and accelerate change. We provide a Global snapshot of each shift, that can impede or enable change in the bullets below

Power

- Phase out unabated coal and fossil gas electricity generation →

- Rapidly scale up zero-carbon electricity generation →

- Modernize power grids, scale energy storage and manage power demand →

- Ensure energy access and a just and equitable transition for all

Industry

- Reduce demand for cement, steel and plastics →

- Improve industrial energy efficiency →

- Electrify industry →

- Commercialize new solutions for cement, steel and plastics →

- Reduce methane emissions from oil and gas operations as they are phased down →

- Transport

- Guarantee reliable access to safe and modern mobility →

- Reduce avoidable vehicle and air travel →

- Shift to public, shared and non-motorized transport →

- Transition to zero-carbon cars and trucks →

- Transition to zero-carbon shipping and aviation → Cities and the Built Environment

- Adopt land use strategies that limit urban expansion and increase accessibility

- Optimize building energy use

- Decarbonize heating, cooling and appliances

- Guarantee access to safe, resilient transport and shelter

- Rapidly scale up zero waste outcomes in cities Technological Carbon Removal

Food

- Scale up technological carbon removal →Food area

- Increase crop productivity sustainably and without expanding into natural areas

- Increase livestock productivity sustainably and without

expanding into natural areas

- Increase aquaculture productivity sustainably and without expanding into natural

- Reduce food loss and waste

- Shift to healthier, more sustainable diets for all

- Reduce GHG emissions and all forms of pollution from food systems

- Reduce the harmful impacts of food production on soil, water, and landscape.

Forests and Land Management

- Protect ecosystems on land

- Restore deforested and degraded lands

- Effectively and sustainably manage land

- Sharply reduce pollution

- Halt the overexploitation of wild species on land and ensure that use is sustainable

Water Management

- Dramatically slow the spread of invasive, alien species on land Ocean Management

- Protect marine and coastal ecosystems

- Restore degraded marine and coastal ecosystems

- Sustainably manage marine and coastal ecosystems

- Sharply reduce pollution from all sources

- Halt the overexploitation of estuarine, coastal, and marine species and ensure that use is sustainable

- Dramatically slow the spread of invasive, alien species in marine ecosystems Freshwater Management

- Protect freshwater ecosystems

- Restore degraded freshwater ecosystems

- Sustainably manage freshwater ecosystems

- Improve water quality

- Halt the overexploitation of wild freshwater species and ensure that use is sustainable

- Dramatically slow the spread of invasive, alien freshwater species

- Ensure reliable access to clean water for all Circular Economy

- Increase material efficiency in production

- Decrease overconsumption

- Regenerate material flows

- Extend the useful life of products and materials

- Recycle and recover resources at their highest value

Finance

- Measure, disclose, and manage climate- and nature-related financial risks →

- Scale up public finance for climate and nature →

- Scale up private finance for climate and nature →

- Extend economic and financial inclusion to underserved and marginalized groups →

- Price greenhouse gas emissions and other environmental externalities →

- Eliminate harmful subsidies and financing → New Economics for Climate and Nature

- Scale new economic ideas and narratives

- Supplement GDP with new measures of prosperity

- Shift to new analytical frameworks and tools that better capture system connections and complexity

- Scale-up the adoption of proven or enhanced economic and financial instruments to foster other transitions

Social Inclusion and Equity

- Provide reliable, universal access to basic services and opportunities

- Reduce social and political inequities

- Facilitate a just transition to a net-zero, nature-positive future

- Re-distribute income and wealth to ensure that they are not concentrated in the hands of the very few

Good Governance

- Safeguard environmental rights

- Ensure transparency and access to information

- Ensure accountability and access to justice

- Ensure participatory and inclusive decision-making

- Strengthen International institutions and laws to more effectively respond to crises that transcend National borders

- Strengthen domestic institutions to implement policies effectively

- Create mechanisms to ensure long term targets align with short term policy

- Reduce corruption and strengthen rule of law

- Ensure responsible research, development, and deployment of innovation

Targets can only tell us part of the story: there are many other factors at play that can spark and sustain progress.

To understand the underlying conditions that can accelerate or impede change, we've identified enablers and barriers across 5 systems.

Innovations in Technology, Practices and Approaches in Leadership from Change Agents, Regulation and Incentives, Strong Institutions, Behavior Change and Shifts in Social Norms.

Keys to climate action: How developing countries could drive Global success and local prosperity.

A new narrative needs to capture the interwoven nature of the world's climate and economic development challenges, anchored in the evolving and diverse perspectives of developing countries themselves. It is a framing that underscores the need for urgent investments in adaptation, resilience, and nature to avoid development setbacks while paying heed to the world's narrow window for climate action.

It requires empathy for many developing countries', profound energy conundrum: a tension between the need to expand access for people who need it most while facing pressures to pursue low-carbon opportunities, often in the face of local political and financing headwinds. It implies practical urgency in tackling the broken threads of the International financing system for climate and development.

The Global, rule-based trade regime that has helped pull more than a billion people out of poverty in recent decades is under pressure. Critics blame it for the loss of manufacturing jobs, environmental degradation, and disruptions to supplies of vital goods like food, medicine, and energy.

Geopolitical tensions are rising. As a result, major players are raising barriers to trade and foreign investment while offering subsidies for domestic production.

The question is now facing policymakers, business leaders, and International organizations: Can Globalization be reshaped to accommodate legitimate National concerns while maintaining trade as an engine of green, inclusive, and resilient development? What are the new opportunities for developing countries to leverage trade for development?

How to Overcome- Structural Weaknesses of the Global South

To research on political economy, decarbonization, colonialism, and the financial and agricultural policies it is necessary to facilitate a Global—and just—green transition.

We explain the three structural weaknesses of the Global south, as exploited and perpetuated by the Global north. I think these points are so critical to understanding the failures of Global capitalism and the traps of debt and inflation, they're worth laying out here. Critically, these traps—which create a structural trade deficit—block Global south countries from developing their own renewable economies, inhibiting both the Global, green transition, and equitable development.

1. Food Sovereignty

If a nation does not have control over its food production, it will always be dependent on other nations for importing its food, and thus dependent on Global supply chains, which have been proven weak during the pandemic. And if you're at the mercy of another country in order to feed your people, you don't have the sovereignty to make decisions about the future of your country. Africa, was once the bread basket of Europe, now imports 85% of its food.

Why? Because of the Common Agricultural Policy.

Upon granting nations in Africa their independence, European leaders recognised the danger of Africa's strong position as the world's food supplier. They realised that they needed food sovereignty, because they'd been importing the vast majority of their food from their colonies. In order create, and then maintain, food sovereignty, European nations (along with Australia, the United States and Japan) decided to subsidise the production of crops produced on home soil, ensuring crops produced at home can be sold at a cheaper price, thus outcompeting African products on the market.

However, this also made European products outcompete African products in Africa, rendering the former breadbasket one of the largest food importers in the world. It is simply cheaper to buy European food than pan-African crops.

2. Energy Sovereignty

The case for energy sovereignty has been easily made by Russia's war in Ukraine (alongside arguments to Nationalise exploitative energy companies). Nations dependent on one another and Global supply chains for their energy are vulnerable.

The energy crisis has hit British residents terribly hard, one of the most "advanced" economies in the world, because the government is unwilling to Nationalise companies which have taken advantage of the crisis to widen their profit margins. People in the UK are rationing their energy and heat supply in order to survive financially. Imagine what a lack of energy sovereignty does to developing nations who are even more vulnerable to market whims and corrupt leaders?

3. Low-Value Added Manufacturing

Low-value added manufacturing, or assembly line manufacturing, means the only manufacturing a nation can participate in doesn't add enough value to their economy because they are still importing more than they export. This applies to many developing nations, including much of Africa, who are dependent on importing the machines and parts needed to create and maintain its assembly line.

4. Broken Promises

The Global north is currently extracting $2 trillion annually from the Global south, a number which far outstrips the annual $100 billion in climate finance promised by the Global north at Copenhagen's COP in 2009. OECD countries have fallen short on that paltry promise of funds every year.

Simply, the Global south must be liberated. Not only do these countries deserve the sovereignty to establish their own National futures, the climate crisis is so urgent and catastrophic that we need all hands-on deck to figure it out. The Global south must no longer take the brunt of the Global north's consumption, emissions, demands and fear.

5. Emissions vs Equality

Current International policy calls for cooperation on the climate crisis whilst shackling the majority of the world's brain power and creativity in debt. Leaders warn against industrial development on the other side of the world whilst looking to the market for solutions. Given the evidence of post-colonial strategies deliberately binding the Global south to the Global north's decisions, one can only wonder if, at the heart of Global north policy, is the plan for the world's richest 1% to live like kings at the expense of everyone else.

According to a recent Oxfam report, the carbon footprints of the richest 1% is set to be 30 times greater than the level compatible with the 1.5°C goal of the Paris Agreement by 2030. That's just 80 million people belching out 16% of the world's total emissions. Surviving the climate crisis demands limiting the world's most privileged.

Allowing the Global south to thrive would necessitate dampening our appetite whilst improving the quality of life for 600 million people. Frankly, it's a win-win situation, and it's the only situation in which we create a sustainable future.

The problem is waiting for leaders to see the value in that which doesn't carry a price tag.

Just Transition requires substantial financial resources to support retraining, economic diversification, and community resilience. How can we ensure adequate funding for Just Transition initiatives, particularly in developing countries that face resource constraints? What burden-sharing mechanisms can be established to ensure that developed nations, with historical responsibility for greenhouse gas emissions, contribute their fair share?

Climate Finance: Central but Insufficient

NDCs are essentially the climate action plans that countries submit under the Paris Climate Agreement. These plans outline the promises countries make to reduce their carbon and greenhouse gas emissions and combat Climate Change. NDCs have two components:

1. Unconditional contributions: These are the actions a country commits to achieving on its own, using its resources and capabilities. For example, mandatory carbon pricing mechanisms, such as carbon taxes or emissions trading systems, typically operate within this space. These contributions reflect what a country believes it can achieve without external assistance.

2. Conditional contributions: These represent additional actions that a country can take if it receives external support, such as climate finance or technology transfer. These commitments rely on cooperation and resource mobilization at the International level.

The unconditional part forms the baseline effort, reflecting not only a country's domestic conditions but also external factors like the actions of other nations. The conditional part instead represents a pathway to higher ambition, very likely made possible only through Global collaboration.

Some criticize International carbon trading as a 'false solution', arguing that it might enable countries to outsource their emission reductions, potentially doing less domestically. This concern is valid if International carbon trading lacks transparency and is poorly integrated into a country's NDC. However, Article 6.4 aims to address these issues by enhancing transparency and accountability in International carbon markets. If a country's unconditional contributions lack sufficient ambition, International carbon trading could become a mechanism to avoid hard choices at home, undermining Global efforts to reduce emissions.

However, the criticism should not be directed at International carbon trading itself or mechanisms like Article 6. The issue lies in the design and ambition of a country's NDC, particularly its unconditional contributions. Sceptics should focus on ensuring that countries establish ambitious, proportionate, and context-appropriate unconditional targets before utilizing International carbon trading as a tool for further action.

Chapter 6 - What Role do Governments, Businesses and Industries Play in Promoting a Just Transition

Finance and Investment

The Finance and Investment theme brings diverse actors together to discuss core issues for financing resilience, covering debt distress and climate and nature action, risk perceptions and rules for finance access, finance mechanisms and means for promoting transparency and accountability. To truly transform climate finance, people and communities that are at the frontlines of Climate Change must be the ones designing new systems.

Develop different types of climate finance and shared understandings of how risk is carried in a financing process, the different ways of channeling finance (and the relationships between different actors involved throughout), and how to ensure finance is transparent and accountable both up and down the chain.

There is a massive funding gap for climate adaptation. The UNEP 2024 Adaptation Gap Report estimates that adaptation needs are 5-10 times greater than current International adaptation investment flows, and the gap is growing. Stakeholders from the financial sector of private finance play a critical role in bridging the adaptation finance gap with specific contributions of commercial banks in financing climate adaptation projects, technologies, and solutions within EMDEs.

Crossing the climate chasm: Catalyzing and scaling innovation ecosystems for inclusive climate resilience

From catalytic innovation to commercial scale, private, non-profit and public actors are coming together to employ fintech solutions to strengthen climate resilience for vulnerable communities across the Global South. What are the critical enablers, best practices and lessons learned from the field? What are the barriers and opportunities ahead to spark more innovative ideas and support enterprises.

Pre-Arranged Financing (PAF) for disasters has the potential to significantly increase the predictability, speed and effectiveness of responses to shocks. Despite gathering momentum, PAF remains a small and niche component of International crisis financing and climate adaptation and resilience building efforts. Meanwhile, exposure to risk continues to grow at alarming rates with countries increasingly experiencing shocks.

Bridging Finance and Biodiversity for Inclusive Locally-Led Climate Action

Climate Change is a multifaceted crisis that demands a cohesive effort to mobilize financial resources, harness cutting-edge solutions, and leverage biodiversity as a foundation for sustainability. The interplay between finance and biodiversity offers a potent opportunity to address Climate Change comprehensively and drive lasting positive outcomes. Connecting climate finance with local communities enhances the efficient allocation of financial resources for climate-resilient projects, ensuring that the unique needs and circumstances of local communities are thoroughly taken into account and integrated into sustainable development strategies. Explore the financing of nature-based solutions for locally-led climate action and address matters such as engagement with the financial sector and private sector together with financial disclosure.

Measuring what we value, or valuing what we measure? Delving into the frontiers of resilience evidence and measurement Over the last decade, resilience has continued to be elevated as an analytic, programmatic, and organizing concept in the climate and development discourse and practice. Approaches to measuring resilience have proliferated, giving rise to a nascent evidence base on the impact of resilience programming that explain why some households, communities, systems, and countries fare better in the face of shocks and stresses than others.

The demand for resilience evidence has also grown exponentially as conflict, Covid-19, and the accelerating impacts of Climate Change have reversed development gains on a massive scale and pushed hundreds of millions of people into crisis levels of poverty and hunger. As we're seeing an increase in financial commitments to adaptation and resilience, it is key to review what works, what doesn't, and how we can tell the difference between the two when it comes to building resilience. Resilience evidence and measurement to address the key demands and concerns of key users for policy, practice and investment.

Green Accountability: Amplifying citizen voices for equitable and effective climate finance Innovative Approaches for Scaling up Investment in Adaptation and Resilience

Bring together different perspectives from financial institutions, bilateral donors, and governments on financing adaptation and resilience. With the goal of supporting communities and countries to become more resilient to future changes in climate, we bring together experts and representatives from across sectors who are rethinking their approaches to addressing risks and scaling up financing for a resilient future.

From Risk to Reward: The Business Imperative to Finance Climate Adaptation & Resilience Financing climate adaptation and resilience is not only a business imperative, but also an opportunity for the private sector to build resilience in ways that benefit both them and the communities, economies, and ecosystems upon which their business models depend.

Disaster Risk Management and Humanitarian Action

The humanitarian consequences of Climate Change are already affecting the lives and livelihoods of millions of people around the world, with the most marginalised and vulnerable communities impacted most severely. Climate-and weather-related disasters, like floods, landslides, storms, droughts, heatwaves and cold spells, are becoming more frequent and intense and lead to cascading social, environmental and economic impacts.

Ecosystems can help to prevent disaster and reduce impacts of disasters on people, critical infrastructure and services. They can also build local socio-ecological resilience against disasters by sustaining livelihoods and providing important products to local populations in times of crises. Socio-ecological resilience is defined as "the capacity to adapt or transform in the face of change in social-ecological systems, particularly unexpected change, in ways that continue to support human well- being"

Enhancing Disaster and Climate Resilience of Infrastructure through Resilience Standards Infrastructure, Energy and Mobility As Climate Change continues to pose significant challenges, codes and standards centered around climate resilience are exerting a transformative influence on the realms of transport infrastructure, energy systems, and mobility solutions. A resilient system is closely interconnected and interdependent on other systems. Coordinated policies and strategies align energy and transport infrastructure resilience goals, creating a more coherent response to climate challenges. Climate data enables these systems to benchmark specifications, integrate innovation, develop data-informed policies and establish standards in planning, design, and operations.

1. Theme Lead - Cities and Urbanization

Nearly 1 billion people – one in four urban dwellers – live in urban slums and informal settlements, making them particularly vulnerable to the consequences of Climate Change, such as droughts and floods. As the Climate Change pressure in those communities increases and the world's cities become a refuge for many, building urban resilience requires understanding the responsibilities across sectors and stakeholders and the range of interdependencies among them. This is needed to deliver climate justice to the most affected, ensure urban equity by integrating diverse urban resilience indicators while strengthening local capacity, facilitating experience sharing, and securing finance for practical approaches to scale existing solutions, as currently only 9% of urban climate investments flow to Climate Change adaptation projects. Financing the replication and scaling up of community-driven innovative strategies, approaches, finance mechanisms, and technologies.

Globally, cities are home to half of the world's people. While cities are growing, the number of people living in urban poverty is increasing. The convergence of rapid urbanization and Climate Change has plunged disadvantaged groups into more vulnerability. Currently, over a billion people are residing in informal settlements and the figure is set to double by 2050. Case studies to highlight how the resilience capacity of informal settlements have been enhanced using grassroot and women-led driven approaches. With a particular focus on triggering further reflection on replication and scaling up, particular focus will be directed on key challenges and enables as well as exploring potential pathways that can help achieve scaling up and sustainable replication of demonstrated pilots

Co-creating Equitable Cities: Catalysts for just climate action Cities and Urbanization

Our cities are inherently unequal, and this inequity is exacerbated by the climate crisis, where marginalized communities bear the brunt of climate impacts. However, there's a shift underway. Climate planning and practice are evolving to become more inclusive, centering equity to disrupt this inequitable burden. We are moving towards fully engaging communities as meaningful partners to co-create and accelerate responses to the climate crisis. A collaborative exploration of how we, as a collective of diverse urban practitioners, can effect this change together. Various communities of practice, from government officials and planners to frontline communities, as well as the organizations and institutions that support them can develop strategies, solutions, and innovations that will drive equitable and climate-resilient urban futures.

Science to Action: Driving Just, Community-Led Transformation Cities & Urbanization

The IPCC's 7th Assessment Report Cycle (AR7) will play a pivotal role in advancing scientific knowledge, driving investment priorities, and guiding our approach to the multitude of challenges we face during the crucial "Decisive Decade". But not everyone has access to the best available science, nor is its delivery always in a form that is easily usable by practitioners. By translating complex climate science into understandable and actionable information, policymakers, businesses, communities, and individuals can make informed decisions and take concrete steps to mitigate and adapt to the climate crisis.

Climate, Housing and Health: How to build inclusive and equitable urban resilience Cities and Urbanization Cities beckon with promises of progress and prosperity. Yet, they grapple with a growing roster of challenges—climate disasters, socio-economic disparities, and health crises—amidst unprecedented environmental shifts. Marginalized communities bear the brunt of these challenges. Urban resilience stands as our beacon, equipping cities to withstand shocks and adapt to chronic stresses, shaping proactive, inclusive communities. At its core, a dynamic nexus converges: climate, housing, and health. Climate Change intensifies extreme events, while housing quality and equity influence health outcomes. Explore innovative solutions, guiding toward cities that are resilient, equitable, and primed for a promising future.

2. Theme Lead - Infrastructure, Energy and Mobility

Developing resilient infrastructure that integrates the changing nature of risk, and the changing needs and demands of communities across the globe calls for looking beyond the physical condition of infrastructure to consider the quality and continuity of services, life-cycle costs including long-term operations and maintenance and loss and damage, as well as

end-of-service-life considerations. A future-ready, just energy transition will reflect in infrastructure that is resilient, sustainable, and people-centered; that builds systemic resilience and tackles interconnected risks; considers nature-based solutions along with hardened structures; provides equitable access to essential services and is predominantly based on clean energy sources. Giving a voice to communities at different stages of infrastructure development, working with nature, revising standards, and adopting certifications will play a significant role in building climate adaptation and resilience as well as combating the exacerbated climate impacts, we are already experiencing.

Revolutionizing Resilience: Harnessing Infra-Tech for climate adaptation Infrastructure, Energy and Mobility Funding and financing infrastructure projects, with those developing and financing Infra-Tech solutions to showcase the potential pipeline for Infra-Tech projects, and proven solutions with the potential to scale across sectors or jurisdictions.

Engineering Action: Influencing the future of the built & natural environment Infrastructure, Energy and Mobility Recognizing that engineers are critical to building resilient & sustainable infrastructure, this session will explore the UNDRR Principles for Resilient Infrastructure and showcase tangible examples of engineering-led transformative action, including practical capacity building of early career engineers.

Making Nature-based Solutions Viable for Multilateral & Private Sector Financing Infrastructure, Energy and Mobility How to accelerate the implementation of nature-based solutions, including green-gray infrastructure at scale – designing and building the next generation of resilient infrastructure to reduce flood risk for up to 680 million people in the coastal zone, providing biodiversity and adaptation benefits as well as a pathway to a low-carbon future.

Green Works and Nature-Based Solutions to Address Climate and Nature Crises -

Locally-led Climate Change adaptation plays a key role in providing green works-

Some 1.2 billion jobs in sectors such as farming, fisheries, forestry and tourism are dependent on the effective management and sustainability of healthy ecosystems. Half of the world's Gross Domestic Product is, to a greater or lesser degree, dependent on nature.

Climate Change and other forms of environmental degradation have therefore negative impacts not only on ecosystems, but also on jobs, economies, and livelihoods. Millions of people are already experiencing higher temperatures and extreme weather events, such as heat waves, droughts, and increased flooding, which are putting food security, water supply and jobs at risk. Vulnerable groups, especially in developing countries, will suffer the most from the changing weather patterns, not only because they are more exposed to climate-related impacts, but also because they have less access to social and financial support, including social protection.

A just transition is not only about the transition of the workforce, for example from fossil fuels industry to renewable energy, but it is equally about supporting developing countries and the most vulnerable to adapt their economies, labour markets and infrastructure to the effects of Climate Change and environmental problems.

Green works in forestry, transport, agriculture and construction sectors have the potential to create highly labor-intensive employment for the vulnerable groups, while contributing to climate and biodiversity goals.

How to effectively explore the design and implementation of green works initiatives to transition to a greener and more resilient society. The most pressing issues on Climate Change adaptation, biodiversity loss and ecosystem degradation, social and environmental safeguards, nature-based solutions and green works for different sectors-

- Learning Block 1 on Climate Change and the rationale for green works

- Learning Block 2 on Climate Change adaptation through biodiversity restoration, including forestry works

- Learning Block 3 on Climate Change adaptation through flood control and rural transport enhancement

- Learning Block 4 on Climate Change adaptation through water management and soil and water conservation

3. Theme Lead -Oceans and Coasts

A healthy ocean and resilient coastal communities are two sides of the same coin. Lives and livelihoods in coastal communities are dependent on a healthy ocean and thriving marine ecosystems. Coastal communities are on the frontline of Climate Change worldwide. Extreme weather events, sea level rise, adverse and significant ecosystem changes, pollution, overfishing, rising levels of acidity, increases in the salinity of freshwater and groundwater, all jeopardise the health of the Ocean and the people who depend on it. These systemic changes put at severe risk the social cohesion of coastal communities leading to migration and population displacement.

Raising Global ambition on the role of the ocean in climate action is critical. It must happen together with accelerating the investment of public, philanthropic, and private capital to implement ocean-climate solutions.

Maritime Resilience: The crucial role of ports in building a more resilient & sustainable future

Concrete examples of the role that ports play as gateways for connecting and catalysing transformation across essential impact systems.

Climate action initiatives undertaken by ports since the launch of the Maritime Resilience Breakthroughs at COP27, contributing to the development of resilient, net-zero futures.

Sustainable Seas: How Improving Fisheries Prevents Conflict Around the World How can we prevent the next conflict over fish?

Pushed by rising temperatures and changing ocean cycles, over half of the world's fish populations are likely to leave their historic habitats by the end of the century. As fishing grounds shift, reliance on the oceans for food increase, and maritime borders move with sea level change, experts expect the number of conflicts over fish to rise.

Water and Nature Resilience in the Climate Era: Innovative, holistic and effective governance Sustainable water and nature governance within an increasingly unstable climate.

Healthy ecosystems are vital for resilience and for guaranteeing human rights. Water is integral to all ecosystems, catalyzing economic growth and sustainable development. Managing and restoring natural ecosystems entails transcending jurisdictional boundaries, breaking down siloed methods, and removing barriers to inclusive, multi-Sectoral cooperation.

Effective, inclusive water governance is crucial for water security and safe drinking water for all. Participation is central to water and nature governance. How youth and indigenous communities' involvement can enhance resilience and address structural inequalities. Investing In Resilient Coastal Communities

Oceans and Coasts: Coastal and marine ecosystems protect communities from ocean risks like storm surge, sequester carbon, support biodiversity, and underpin blue economy sectors. Globally, these ecosystems are under threat. Governments, the private sector, and civil society must partner to drive investment into regenerating ocean natural capital and building resilient coastal communities. This will require developing innovative financial products, particularly for Small Island Developing States (SIDS) and coastal Least Developed Countries (LDCs), to scale conservation and restoration and enable an inclusive, equitable, and sustainable blue economy.

4. Theme Lead -Arts, Culture, Antiquities, and Heritage

Culture, from art to heritage, empowers people to imagine and realise a low-carbon, just, climate resilient future. Between technological innovation and individual choice lies the communal realm, a social world of remembering, creating, sharing, and belonging that binds people to places and to each other.

Traditional knowledge, culture, and heritage are often not acknowledged, nor validated in climate action and policy. Local and social knowledge, often expressed through cultural experiences and values, already have the building blocks for resilience and adaptation, yet this has not been understood generally. Through community-centred approaches, culture-based strategies strengthen resilience by supporting social networks and diverse knowledge systems and practices.

Artivism for a Resilient Future: Democratising science and amplifying alternative voices through art Indigenous, traditional, and local knowledge, culture, and heritage are often not acknowledged, nor validated in climate research, action and policy. Marginalised groups often are not included in the decision making process, and those knowledges that are often expressed through art, cultural experiences, and values have not been understood generally.

On the other hand, art has the potential to cut across disciplinary, socio-economic, linguistic and Educational differences. Art is a shared language that could amplify alternative voices, makes cultures visible, audible, and tangible and able to communicate climate impacts from multiple vantage points for climate justice and a resilient future.

Preserving Our Legacy: Climate Resilience for Culture and Heritage

Voices from frontline communities to share their climate action stories. A new method of evaluating non-economic loss and damage, cultural centered climate vulnerability assessments, community-engaged training to show how putting people in the center of solutions helps drive ambition to meet the urgency before us.

5. Theme Lead -Health and Wellbeing

Building on the conversations at recent COPs the aim is to galvanise action across the health, climate and urban nexus, helping people in these fields create the space for collaboration and the locally applicable tools needed to accelerate and unlock transformative changes.

The Health and Wellbeing theme will take a systems approach and further illuminate the interconnectivity between human health and Climate Change both in terms of shared challenges but also shared solutions. Focusing on expanding the dialogue to a broader set of actors who may not be considered as a part of the traditional health care system but who provide critical contributions and insight into how we address health and wellbeing in the face of the climate crisis. Explore the existing data available to inform health and climate resilience programs, the impacts of Climate Change on labour productivity, and health implications of plans and early warning systems as they relate to rising temperatures and extreme heat events.

Voices from the Ground: Building climate-resilient health systems through locally-led action Ways in which community-level activities – from strengthening health systems to locally-led adaptation, as well as examples of indigenous and community-led interventions – have created opportunities to improve the resilience of health systems. Embedding community-led actions and principles, prioritizing programming principles to build climate-resilient health systems, as well as implications for governance, National policies, and planning/management strategies.

Psychological Resilience as a Pillar for Climate Resilience

Interactions between health and climate adaptation have huge potential to address the future of Global health. Health and wellbeing are recognized in the Adaptation Agenda and by increasing areas of climate adaptation as a key "system" that needs International investment and action as part of meaningful and substantive climate resilience and climate justice impacts.

Psychological resilience, and mental and emotional wellbeing, are critical for such potential impacts. But that will require a paradigm shift—markedly enlarging how to understand what psychological resilience means, who owns it, and how to do it, in ways that moves far beyond just illness categories and care, to empower and enable social capital, collective efficacy, and, especially locally led, climate adaptation. A Roadmap for spreading psychological resilience through the Race to Resilience, decades of evidence and practice to draw on but also substantially build upon from the field of Global mental health, and examples of connecting these efforts to climate solidarity and justice.

Addressing the Nexus of Women, Climate Change and Health through Governance, Accountability and Innovative Finance

Addressing the intertwined challenges of health and climate impact on marginalized communities, this initiative advocates for governance, accountability, and innovative financing. It emphasizes cross-sector collaboration, gender-inclusive policies, and community engagement. Local adaptation efforts prioritize dual-purpose projects that empower women, and innovative financing models seek to bridge disparities. A knowledge-sharing platform informs data-driven strategies. This holistic approach strives to safeguard the health and livelihoods of those most vulnerable to Climate Change, fostering resilience and sustainability.

How do Government strengthen Monetary Policy Frameworks?

Here are some ways monetary policy can be used to promote economic transformation and sustainable development.

Green Financing –

Monetary policy can be used to promote green financing, which supports environmentally sustainable economic activity. Central banks can use their regulatory and supervisory powers to encourage financial institutions to increase their lending to green projects and reduce their exposure to carbon-intensive activities.

Inflation Targeting –

Inflation targeting can promote sustainable development by stabilizing prices and reducing the uncertainty associated with inflation. This can encourage long-term investment and support sustainable economic growth. However, it is crucial to understand the underlying cause of the inflation. Monetary tightening may make things worse if inflation is caused by supply shocks rather than excess demand.

Sustainable Finance Frameworks –

Monetary policy frameworks can also be used to develop sustainable finance frameworks that promote investment in sustainable infrastructure and social projects. These could include, for instance, requirements upon financial institutions to ensure compliance with the Environmental, Social, and Governance factors when making investment or lending decisions.

Green Bond Purchases –

Central banks can purchase green bonds to support the development of sustainable infrastructure and finance projects that reduce carbon emissions. This can increase the supply of green bonds in the market and encourage more investors to invest in sustainable projects.

Improved Policy Coordination

- Collaboration between monetary authorities, governments, and other stakeholders can help to promote sustainable development and transformation of the economy through a common understanding of the medium to long-term development plans and coordinated policy decisions.

- The achievement of the Sustainable Development Goal 3 - health and well-being depends on the achievement of many other goals related to the environment, development, equity or justice. But it is clear that for the moment there are still weaknesses and gaps in the consideration of the links between health and environment as a whole.

- Challenge is no longer to mobilize actors for the success of each SDG, but also to recognize their interdependence and to create networks of actors capable of contributing to the achievement of the health, justice and environmental SDGs. The post-COVID19 strategies will help us to bridge this integration gap.

- For each SDG, as in the case of the health and well-being goal, it is a question of identifying mobilizing the research, political and private actors capable of responding to the research, innovation and development challenges that will enable the health goals to be implemented. It is therefore a question of identifying, mobilizing and networking to create a dialogue between actors who would have had little chance of meeting without this effort to implement each SDG.

- The "One Health" approach is based on the need to understand health in its multiple aspects and components through shared health like animal health, ecosystem health - while the "Global health" approach is based on the principle that reducing Global impacts and Global changes can contribute to Global human health. Global health has developed within an alliance, the Global Health Alliance, which was officially launched in 2021 and is a consortium of universities, NGO's research institutes and other entities from around the world committed to understanding and addressing Global environmental change i.e. the health of the planet itself but also to its impacts on human health.

- According to the Global Health Alliance, Global health is a transdisciplinary field and a solution-oriented social movement focused on analyzing and resolving the impacts of human disturbance on the Earth's natural systems and ultimately on human health and on all life on Earth. It is now a question of articulating the one health and planetary health but also Global health in order to effectively address socio-economic environmental, biodiversity, and health issues, and thus promote their implementation in biosphere reserves.

An increasing number of countries are taking steps to develop One Health coordination mechanisms to support multi-Sectoral surveillance especially at the interface between human health and veterinary health, laboratory capacity, and risk assessment, communication and policy making activities, including inter Sectoral policy making, between the human and animal health sectors.

The Anthropocene is the new era defined by human impacts on the planet. Indeed, through its action on the ecosystems and the climate, humanity has become a geological force. Planetary health offers an integrative approach linking human health this time with Global planetary functioning. Both approaches result in concrete and successful recommendations that complement each other perfectly.

One health" is not the only aspect of making this connection between biodiversity, environment and human health. Planetary health starts from the notion of the Anthropocene and its 9 planetary boundaries, the crossing of which could upset the functioning of the planet as a whole. The 9 planetary boundaries include Climate Change, the ozone layer, geochemical cycles, ocean acidification and the integrity of the biosphere. This new approach differs essentially from the "One Health" approach in the angle of vision and therefore in the practical applications.

Policymakers need to improve fiscal positions and sustainability to ensure they can effectively respond to the next downturn. To achieve more sustainable fiscal positions, policies must minimize the negative short-term consequences of fiscal consolidation on economic activity to the extent possible. This requires safeguarding critical poverty-reducing expenditures, implementing growth-enhancing spending, and implementing tax reforms that promote investment and revenue mobilization.

However, it is important to apply policies to reduce that effect and converge to equality from the beginning onwards. This shape is commonly known as the Kunetz curve, which looks like a reversed U, but there are many arguments on how this could be prevented and it is actually not an economic law at all as many think.

Leveraging in-Country Collaboration

It is not difficult to see how in-country collaboration can be a catalyst for progress across all the SDGs. A critical step in achieving goals related to climate and nature, for example, is the rapid adoption of renewable energy. Governments have introduced incentives that encourage the private sector to invest in both proven and emerging renewable energy technologies. These country-specific collaborations have yielded low-cost, high-quality renewable energy solutions for consumers, contributing to a large-scale shift across society that wouldn't otherwise be possible.

When it comes to driving progress on health care, NGOs and foundations can partner with both governments and health care companies to improve the delivery of in-country health care services to communities in need. This also applies to pandemic preparedness and response.

During the COVID-19 pandemic, for example, public-private partnerships helped to dramatically scale and speed up vaccine testing, production, and distribution.

The opportunities for such cross-sector cooperation to drive SDGs, and social and economic progress more generally, are many. But to seize them, we must radically rethink how we collaborate and then develop and implement the best country-level collaboration models.

Digital Transformation Can Accelerate Progress on the SDGs

While progress on the Sustainable Development Goals has been slow thus far, digital technologies can be a game changer. Initial BCG analysis shows 70% of the 169 SDG targets have already been impacted by digital solutions. And the impact of digital goes beyond individual use cases: when comparing within the same income group, countries with advancements in digital infrastructure realize up to 40% faster progress on the SDGs.

To reap the greatest benefit from digital technologies, however, countries will need to move beyond pushing one SDG-related digital initiative, or even a series of them, and instead develop a comprehensive digital strategy aligned with National development goals.

Assessing the Link Between Digital and SDG Progress

Assessing digital technologies' SDG impact is complex, and it's made more challenging by the limited availability of data and the multifaceted nature of both digital and SDG progress. Despite these obstacles, our empirical assessment points towards the great potential of digital technologies for advancing the SDGs.

BCG's analysis examined the relationship between SDG progress (as reflected in the UN Sustainable Development Solutions Network's SDG Index) and digital maturity. To assess digital maturity, we looked at the Telecommunications Infrastructure Index (a proxy for digital infrastructure) and the data-only mobile broadband basket (a proxy for digital affordability).

Countries that have made considerable progress on digital infrastructure or affordability—were found to achieve up to 40% more progress on the SDGs compared with peer countries in their income group. Digging into the two components of digital maturity, we found-

- Digital Infrastructure. Lower- and middle-income countries with stronger growth in infrastructure (the top 20%) realized 40% more progress across all SDGs from 2010 to 2020. High-income countries did even better, showing a 44% increase in progress.

- Digital Affordability. Countries in the top 40% of digital affordability among high-income countries achieved 58% more progress across all SDGs from 2014 to 2020.

- To better understand the relationship between digital leadership and SDG progress, existing digital technologies can support SDG progress across nations by fulfilling two primary functions: empowering marginalized groups and enabling better efficiency and monitoring of the environment.

- For instance, some digital technologies support financial inclusion, Education access, and market entry, empowering marginalized people and advancing certain SDGs, including #1 (No Poverty), #2 (Zero Hunger), #4 (Quality Education), and #5 (Gender Equality). Others, such as algorithmic-driven water management and sensors that monitor the health of endangered ecosystems, enhance decision making, boosting SDGs #13 (Climate Action), #14 (Life Below Water), and #15 (Life on Land). The Need for a Holistic Strategy National governments should drive progress on digital maturity and underlying digital transformations, yet all stakeholders must collaborate to ensure inclusive digital transformation and SDG success.

- We see four major step changes that can be driven through action by all members of the International development community:

- Scale proven digital solutions. The focus should be on moving beyond pilots and scaling proven cross border digital solutions. These efforts must be designed to foster interoperability and data collection so that assessments of the impact of digital can be done efficiently and effectively.

- Improve collaboration and raise ambition among stakeholders. Digital transformation demands joint efforts between private-sector players, financial institutions, civil society, UN agencies, and governments. Taking an "all Handson deck" approach ensures the acceleration of digital progress at both National and Global levels.

- Expand funding and financing approaches. Closing the $3.7 trillion-plus SDG funding gap requires concerted actions, including the pooling of resources through collaboration and the leveraging of methods such as blended finance.

- Unlock private-sector potential for greater societal impact. The private sector's pivotal SDG role hinges on concrete ESG pledges, open innovation, Global collaboration, and supply chain decarbonization. Strengthening incentives and implementing guardrails can help channel those efforts.

Fulfilling the UN's 2030 Agenda is a promise every member state of the UN has made. Digital technologies offer a way to leap ahead in SDG progress today, improving the quality of life of humans. Every country should seize this opportunity.

Climate Change will almost certainly influence policy across all sectors of the World economy. However, macroeconomic modeling, which informs budgeting all the way up to the state level and therefore the direction of the entire economy, does not yet account for the impacts of Climate Change. The question is how economists can better incorporate physical climate risks into macroeconomic models.

We now know the economic impacts of the climate and nature crises are accelerating at an unprecedented rate. This is a direct financial and strategic challenge that is already reshaping markets, disrupting supply chains, and intensifying competition for scarce resources.

Such disruption calls for the need for a competitive edge – one enabled by close collaboration between businesses and policymakers in order to foster demand and incentivise innovation.

A follow up to Survival of the Fittest: From ESG to Competitive Sustainability. This new landmark business briefing should offer a pathway for the private sector to accelerate market-wide transition, to innovate and prepare to compete on a level playing field that will reward superior sustainability performance.

References

https://www.lse.ac.uk/granthaminstitute/publication/Global-trends-in-climate-change-litigation-20 23-snapshot/

https://lnkd.in/e9tdVbiA

https://napcentral.org/#

https://www.c40knowledgehub.org/s/topic/0TO1Q000000UBYYWA4/economic-tools-for-climate-action?language=en_US

https://systemschangelab.org/

https://www.un.org/sites/un2.un.org/files/Global_accelerator_summary.pdf

giggabox.eventsair.com

unclimatesummit.org

www.eticanews.it

www.bcg.com

cleenet.org

www.planetcritical.com

cgspace.cgiar.org

systemschangelab.org

euagenda.eu

gunungcapital.com

www.Globalgovernmentforum.com

docslib.org